T0266816

FOUCAULT IN
CALIFORNIA

FOUCAULT IN
CALIFORNIA

[A True Story—Wherein the Great French
Philosopher Drops Acid in the Valley of Death]

Simeon Wade

Foreword by Heather Dundas

HEYDAY

Heyday, Berkeley, California

Copyright © 2019 by David Wade; original copyright © 1990 by Simeon Wade
Foreword © 2019 by Heather Dundas

All rights reserved. No portion of this work may be reproduced or transmitted in any form or by any means, electronic or mechanical, including photocopying and recording, or by any information storage or retrieval system, without permission in writing from Heyday.

The Library of Congress has cataloged the hardcover edition as follows:
Names: Wade, Simeon, 1940- author.
Title: Foucault in California : a true story--wherein the great French philosopher drops acid in the Valley of Death / Simeon Wade ; foreword by Heather Dundas.
Description: Berkeley, CA : Heyday, 2019.
Identifiers: LCCN 2018033461 (print) | LCCN 2018050013 (ebook) | ISBN 9781597144728 (E-book) | ISBN 9781597144636 (hardcover)
Subjects: LCSH: Foucault, Michel, 1926-1984. | LSD (Drug)
Classification: LCC B2430.F724 (ebook) | LCC B2430.F724 W33 2019 (print) | DDC 194--dc23
LC record available at https://lccn.loc.gov/2018033461

Cover Design: Ashley Ingram
Interior Design/Typesetting: Ashley Ingram
Cover Image: © Gabriel Alcala, originally published in *The Baffler*, issue no. 46

Published by Heyday
P.O. Box 9145, Berkeley, CA 94709
(510) 549-3564
heydaybooks.com

Printed by Lightning Source, USA

10 9 8 7 6 5 4 3 2

CONTENTS

FOREWORD

HEATHER DUNDAS

In *The Lives of Michel Foucault*, David Macey quotes Foucault as speaking "nostalgically...of 'an unforgettable evening on LSD, in carefully prepared doses, in the desert night, with delicious music, nice people, and some chartreuse.'" This "unforgettable evening" took place in 1975, when Foucault, then a visiting professor at the University of California at Berkeley, was driven to Death Valley by an assistant professor at Claremont Graduate School and his boyfriend, a pianist. Once there, the two young men persuaded Foucault to experience the desert night under the influence of a psychedelic drug. This was Foucault's first experience with acid, and by the morning, he was crying and proclaiming that he knew Truth.

I first heard this story in 2014, when I was a graduate student at the University of Southern California. I found it frankly hard to believe that a philosopher of Foucault's standing would have had the time to take a trip with two strangers, and even harder to believe that he would, at age forty-nine, agree to experiment with psychedelic drugs with these strangers. The whole episode was absurd, I thought, and it triggered something deeply snarky in me. I hated "theory." I hated Foucault, who seemed to embody all the privilege and arrogance of the theory movement. When I heard that Foucault's host in Death Valley, Simeon Wade, had an unpublished manuscript describing this experience in the desert, I decided to track him down. I wanted to get Wade's manuscript and use it to write a satire about idiot academics in the desert.

I badgered someone who knew someone who had his address. "He's a recluse," the friend of a friend said. "Doesn't use a computer or a phone, and basically lives off the grid."

I wrote Wade a letter introducing myself and asking for a meeting. He sent back a postcard with a date, a time, and the address of a Starbucks near his home in Oxnard, California—about sixty-five miles from Pasadena, where I live.

"How will I know it's him?" I asked my source.

"You'll know," he replied.

And I did. Half an hour after the appointed time, as I was getting ready to leave, a twenty-five-year-old pickup truck rattled into the podmall parking lot. The driver sat for a moment finishing a cigarette before gathering up half a dozen plastic grocery bags and an armload of books. A tall and heavyset man, he wore an electric-blue T-shirt half-tucked into a pair of baggy farmer jeans. Upon entering the Starbucks, he walked straight to me and dropped the bags and the books on the table where I sat. He doffed his emerald-green baseball cap, revealing a bald head sprinkled with age spots.

"Delighted to meet you," he said, a trace of Texas in his accent. His words were as soft and whispered as Gaelic, and I realized with some alarm that he had no teeth. "I've brought you some reference material and an icy cold Coke for your drive home."

He sat down and started telling tales that I found hard to believe. Oh yes, he had taken Michel Foucault to Death Valley. Foucault, Wade said, had loved this trip so much that he had called it one of the most important experiences of his life. But that was only the beginning of their association; Foucault had visited him several times. Wade had interviewed Foucault on television at Claremont Graduate School. Foucault had written to him to say that he'd burned a completed early manuscript of one volume of *The History of Sexuality* as a direct result of his experience in Death Valley. Foucault had been at work on a manuscript about monsters during one of his visits "because he always thought he was a monster."

Wade claimed that he and Foucault remained friends for the rest of Foucault's life—and that there was a photograph in *Time* magazine to prove it. Indeed, Foucault had written to ask his dear friend Simeon to bring more LSD to him in Paris in 1984, when he was dying. "Michel wanted to go out tripping, like Aldous Huxley," Wade said.

In response to my bug-eyed question he snapped that *yes,* he had written a manuscript about this, but no one was interested in publishing it.

Could I see it?

Wade looked at me suspiciously. His manuscripts were somewhere deep in one of his four storage units, he said, along with the photographs and letters from Foucault. They were hard to get to. Someday, he said, he would show them to me. If I came back. If he could find them. Maybe.

So would he meet with me again?

He would, and we set a date for the following month.

In between our visits, I tried to authenticate the man and his stories. I discovered that Wade was born in 1940 in Enterprise, Alabama. He had earned a B.A. in history from the College of William and Mary in 1962, and then attended Harvard University on a Woodrow Wilson Fellowship, earning his Ph.D. in 1968 on the intellectual history of Western civilization. Wade assumed an assistant professorship at Claremont Graduate School in 1972 and cofounded a doctoral program in European studies there. Photos of Wade at this stage of his life reveal a staggeringly handsome man: tall, athletic, always dressed in a suit and tie.

The European Studies Program was short-lived, and so, apparently, was Wade's career at Claremont. And at this point, the record on Wade got sketchy. I visited Claremont Graduate School to look for tapes of the television program, or some other archival evidence of Foucault's visit, or even records of Simeon Wade's teaching career there. There was no record of Foucault's visit in the CGS archives, and I was only able to document Wade's time at Claremont by searching through old copies of the student newspaper.

I went back to Oxnard the following month and again waited for Wade at Starbucks.

On this day, Wade arrived empty-handed but only twenty minutes late, and he wanted to talk about the value of mind-altering experiences.

"All cultures spring from hallucinogenic mushrooms," he said.

"Think about it. The ancient Greeks, the Aztecs, the Vikings—all had rituals centered on the state of altered consciousness from mushrooms. And what's ritual but a form of religion, and what's religion but a form of culture?"

Oh, man, I thought. This satire writes itself. I requested another meeting the following month.

Wade's primary topic of conversation was Foucault. He considered Foucault to be "the greatest thinker of our time, perhaps of all time[;] to compare him to any other is like lighting a candle in the sunshine." Wade had an encyclopedic knowledge of Foucault's work, and he talked of his friendship with the philosopher as the "second great stroke of luck in my life."

The first great stroke of luck in Wade's life, he told me, was the third person on the trip to Death Valley with Foucault: the pianist Michael Stoneman. Wade met Stoneman in 1974 and they were a couple until Stoneman's death in 1998. Their open cohabitation apparently caused some resentment in the conservative town of Claremont in the 1970s; Wade's brother, David Wade, whom I met much later, recalled, "Simeon didn't just come out; he *came out!*" David told me about Simeon and Michael's shared love of music, and how in one of their houses they had placed a pair of grand pianos head to head in the living room so they could play Arensky duets.

As we continued to meet, Wade started to let me see beyond the persona of Foucault's friend. He said he had known Timothy Leary at Harvard "and he [Leary] was all about orgasms." He spoke of some of the dire consequences visited on a nonconformist in academia in the 1970s: according to Wade, he didn't make tenure at Claremont Graduate School because "they said I was a drug dealer; they said we had orgies; they said I was a madman." He hinted at the dark times he and Michael endured after he left Claremont. Together they ran an art gallery for a while, and then Wade began picking up teaching gigs around Los Angeles. Although he never again held a tenure-track position, Wade taught at California State University at Northridge, Belmont Prep and Belmont College, the Samra University of Oriental Medicine, the Tao Healing Arts Center, and the controversial Pacific Western University. His longest association was with the Otis Art Institute of Parsons School of Design, where he taught history and art history for sixteen years. Eventually he found work as a psychiatric nurse at County/USC Medical Center because he "wanted to work with real madmen." According to David Wade, Simeon and Michael were in increasingly desperate financial peril during this time. Perhaps because of this, or perhaps in tandem with it, both men faced crises in their physical and mental health as well. In 1998, Stoneman died of alcoholism at age forty-seven.

Despite the specificity of Wade's stories, I could find little evidence to support them. Scholarly mentions of the friendship between Wade and Foucault were scant, and, with the exception of details in James Miller's 1993 book *The Passion of Michel Foucault,* generally dismissive. David Macey expresses the general dismissal of a drug-induced epiphany in *The Lives of Michel Foucault,* which was published the same year: "Reports from those who claim that he told them that it changed his life should probably be treated with some skepticism; the insights granted by LSD tend to be short-lived and illusory rather than real." The ongoing friendship between Foucault and Wade was beginning to seem more based on hope than fact. I thought that perhaps Wade was just an old, lonely guy who told tall tales about his one brush with celebrity.

However, evidence began to trickle in. I discovered that there is, in fact, a photograph in *Time* magazine's November 16, 1981, issue of Wade and Stoneman laughing with Foucault outside a conference in 1981. And after we had been meeting for about a year, Wade showed up one day with his manuscript, *Foucault in California*. It was copyrighted 1990, and Wade said that Foucault had read it and approved its publication, but no publishing house would touch it—too scandalous, or perhaps too tainted by its connection with Wade. "This is the only copy left," he said. "I can't let you have it." So we drove together to a copy shop and he watched as I photocopied the pages, one by one.

WADE'S MANUSCRIPT IS as outlandish as I could hope. *Foucault in California* is written in the same high-velocity voice as the fantastical stories Simeon told me over coffee. It describes how the initial idea of an "experiment" with Foucault's mind soon evolved into a premeditated bacchanal, with Wade and Stoneman at the center of the action. Within Wade's enthusiastic description of his Dionysian scheme, sacred and popular references mix: Joanne Woodward as the dissociative personality in the 1957 film *The Three Faces of Eve* compounds with the biblical Eve, and Mussorgsky's 1967 witches' sabbath merges with Stokowski's 1941 interpretation in Disney's *Fantasia*. This high/low fantasy/*Fantasia* provides a glimpse into Wade's bivalent thinking. His writing is exaggerated; his devotion to Foucault is unshakeable.

However, by the time I read the manuscript, I had abandoned my original idea of an exposé of the theory movement. I realized that this territory has already been well covered, satirically and otherwise, by people far more fitted for the task than I am. Scholars have continued to pick through Foucault's work after his death, with waves of books and articles, debates and challenges following each new translation and publication of work from Foucault's immense oeuvre. My feelings about Foucault are unimportant.

Also, I began to take seriously some of what Wade was telling me. While Wade's gonzo manuscript has its funny moments, and it definitely is tempting to mock the drugs at play or use them as a punchline—"Foucault dropping acid in the desert"—this minimizes what Wade, certainly, and Foucault, possibly, were trying to do: expand consciousness, have a limit-experience. Until recently, the very 1970s idea of having, as Wade puts it, a "magic elixir" to expand consciousness was so out of fashion as to be ludicrous. However, current research has called this dismissal of the psychedelic experience into question. The assertion that LSD's effects are "short-lived and illusory" is now being challenged, and therapeutic uses for a long-denigrated substance are now being explored. Perhaps altered consciousness is not (just) a joke.

Finally, and to my surprise, I lost my desire to hold Wade up for ridicule. Instead we became friends, eventually celebrating birthdays and holidays together.

Even so, I was still not fully convinced that his manuscript was any more than the product of an extremely fertile imagination. Then, early in 2016, Wade—"Simeon" to me by then—located a carousel of slides depicting the Death Valley trip. There was Foucault with his arm around a shirtless Michael Stoneman, grinning at Dante's View. In another shot, Foucault gazes off into the distance at Zabriskie Point. "He was tripping his brains out in this one," said Simeon. The images were stunning, but most importantly they were proof, finally, that this trip did happen. In addition, multiple images of Foucault at Simeon and Michael's house in Claremont supported Simeon's assertion that Foucault returned to visit them at least one more time. These snapshots illustrate what Simeon had claimed: he and Foucault were friends.

At this point I began to lobby Simeon to allow me to interview him for publication. It took more than a year for him to agree. When this interview and a few of the images were published in the online journal *Boom California* in September 2017, I drove out to Oxnard to show it to Simeon on my laptop, as he still did not possess a computer of his own.

We met on a Friday, as usual. He was late, of course.

The following Tuesday, October 3, 2017, Simeon died unexpectedly in his sleep. He was seventy-seven years old.

WHILE SORTING THROUGH Simeon's belongings, David Wade and his wife, Nancy Pobanz, uncovered the letters from Foucault, which Simeon had talked about but never could find. These letters reveal that Foucault did indeed claim the night in Death Valley as "a great experience, one of the most important in my life" (May 14, 1975)—and that Foucault had read Simeon's manuscript and responded positively, if gnomically:

Comment aurait-il été possible de ne pas aimer toi[1]

> *Simeon*
> *Death Valley Trip*
> *Epistème la gris*
> (September 16, 1978)

Other letters assert that Foucault was considering larger changes in his life—"I feel that I have to emigrate and become a Californian" (May 30, 1975)—and prove that Foucault and Simeon were in touch until 1984, the year Foucault died. (Unfortunately, David Wade and Nancy Pobanz did not find Foucault's manuscript about monsters. Nor did they find the letter asking Simeon and Michael to come to Paris to help Foucault die.)

At the time of this writing (mid-2018), Simeon's papers are now stacked up in my house, pending their accession into the ONE National Gay and Lesbian Archives at the University of Southern California. And the posthumous publication of the fourth and final volume of Foucault's *History of Sexuality* series, *Confessions of the Flesh* (2018)—

---

1 Foucault's note reads "How would it have been possible to not love you[?]" As for "*Epistème la gris,*" Foucault scholars should have the final word on what it might have meant.

written after Foucault met Simeon, and possibly influenced by their friendship—makes the publication of Simeon's manuscript, *Foucault in California,* especially timely. David Wade and Nancy Pobanz found a letter written a few months after the Death Valley trip in which Foucault says he had to "begin again" on his "book about sexual repression" (October 5, 1975).

Although he was too old and I was too stodgy for my own Death Valley trip, Simeon did once organize an "experience" for me. He placed me in a chair behind a wall of books in his jammed, hoarder-level apartment and handed me a large Cadbury milk bar. I wasn't happy about this: I'm fond of neither clutter nor milk chocolate, and it was getting late and I was worried about my drive home in the dark. Simeon disappeared behind the wall and began playing a Chopin étude. In the dim light of the fading day, my world was reduced to a view of books and the sound of the piano. It was...not relaxing, but perhaps stupefying. At a particularly lovely moment Simeon called, "Eat the chocolate *now!*"

This experience was just a shadow of the immersive event Wade created for Michel Foucault in Death Valley. But now, for me, milk chocolate will always have the resonance of Chopin and the memory of a friend, and my life is richer for it. Furthermore, I now understand how "an...evening on LSD, in carefully prepared doses, in the desert night, with delicious music, nice people, and some chartreuse" could perhaps be one of the most important experiences of a person's life.

Foucault's desert night was an immersion into an experience carefully choreographed by Wade for maximum effect. In Wade's dinner party/performance, Western tropes—of shamans, vision quests, male friendship—were entangled and inverted. Arguably, this absurd night spent with a "madman" peddling LSD and his partner playing Stockhausen embodied Foucault's emerging concept of friendship, a concept he elaborated in some of his last interviews as a type of aesthetics of existence, involving an "art of life." Foucault hinted at this connection when he wrote to Simeon on May 14, 1975, proposing another visit, but only if it was convenient: "I think that such meetings don't make sense if they don't give to everybody an intense and reciprocal pleasure and the same quietness. What we have to do is find the way to make with the 'principe de plaisir' [a] 'principe de realité.' That is, I think, an ethical and a political problem to be solved nowadays."

Wade's manuscript, Foucault in California, allows you to ride along on this Death Valley trip. May your life be richer for it.

Heather Dundas
Pasadena, CA

FOUCAULT IN
CALIFORNIA

We can only think of Plato and Aristotle in grand academic robes. They were honest men, like others, laughing with their friends, and, when they diverted themselves with writing their Laws and the Politics, they did it as an amusement. That part of their life was the least philosophic and the least serious; the most philosophic was to live simply and quietly. If they wrote on politics, it was as if laying down rules for a lunatic asylum; and if they presented the appearance of speaking of a great matter, it was because they knew that the madmen, to whom they spoke, thought they were kings and emperors. They entered into their principles in order to make their madness as little harmful as possible.

—Blaise Pascal, *Pensées*

PROLEGOMENA

One spring day in the mid-seventies, a colleague phoned to tell me that the inestimable Michel Foucault was scheduled to teach a seminar at the University of California in Berkeley. I was jubilant. Michel Foucault was my hero, and at last there was a possibility of meeting him. He was already considered one of the most prominent French intellectuals of the twentieth century. I regarded Michel Foucault as nothing less than the greatest thinker of our time, perhaps of all time. To compare him to any other is like lighting a candle in the sunshine.

It had been nine years since, as a student in intellectual history at Harvard, I had read Foucault's first major work, *Madness and Civilization*. The book excited me in the extreme, but I was not sophisticated enough in my own thinking to comprehend the full implications of its revolutionary import. Certainly I got little help from the professors at Harvard, many of whom were mired in narrow specializations, puerile ideologies, and obsolete methodologies.

By the time I started teaching at Harvard in the late sixties I still took a Hegelian approach to history and literature. Then I read Foucault's *The Order of Things*. I discarded Hegelianism and declared to my students that Foucault's conceptualization of the episteme was for the human sciences the equivalent of Watson and Crick's analysis of the double helix for the life sciences.

After reading *Discipline and Punish* in 1975, I knew that the work of Michel Foucault was the decisive watershed in modern intellectual history. When I read *Anti-Oedipus,* by Foucault's colleagues Gilles Deleuze and Félix Guattari, I felt that together the three of them had answered the most pressing question of our time: "Why fascism and how do we resist it?" In my mind, Foucault and his circle had laid the groundwork for finding out what we really need to know about mind and society. They were articulating the lineaments of a new age that was upon us.

I was so transfigured by Foucault's work that I hungered for information about his life. Initially all I knew about Foucault as a person was derived from the brief account of his teaching career presented on the jacket of *The Order of Things.*

In 1969, when I was living in Paris, I inquired about Foucault from my lover, who was a professor at the Sorbonne. She told me that Foucault belonged to *the* infamous circle of homosexual intellectuals in Paris. "He is one of *them,*" she said contemptuously. However, she deigned to respect his work. When I asked if she agreed with Foucault's politics, she replied that her loyalty to the left was only in terms of lifestyle, nothing more.

Her highness also told me not to bother trying to read Foucault's *Archaeology of Knowledge,* shortly after it appeared in the Parisian bookstores, because it was far beyond my powers of comprehension. The news that Foucault was openly homosexual, the notion that his books were too difficult for a struggling American student, and his reputation as an advocate for the May '68 student uprising in Paris whetted my interest in him even more.

In 1971, Michel Foucault was appointed to one of the most prestigious chairs at the pinnacle of French academia. He was made Professor of the History of Systems of Thought at the Collège de France. The title was literally created for him, for the unique character of his work. In a sense he was the first to apply systems analysis to the history of thought.

We might deem Foucault a systems analyst, even a great philosopher, historian, sociologist, and psychologist, but he actually considered himself a journalist. He studied the past only for the purpose of understanding the present. He analyzed the history of the mind in order to explicate the power of discourse. His statement "We are what has been said" is an apt introduction to his approach to history and the human sciences.

Every Wednesday during the short term at the Collège de France, Foucault read his lecture as he sat in front of a bare table lighted by a single lamp. The hall was always packed with attentive students and peers, many of whom taped each session. It was the same hall where Henri Bergson, the famous philosopher, held forth during the Proustian era. As with Bergson, one had to wait in line to gain admittance to the hall when Michel Foucault spoke. It was always an event.

THE SAME YEAR that Foucault assumed his august chair in Paris I landed a paltry assistant professor's job at the Claremont Graduate School, located in the San Gabriel Valley at the furthermost eastern and conservative fringe of Los Angeles County. The Graduate School is part of a cluster of institutions known as the Claremont Colleges. The School and the Colleges are located in a smug, churchy, Midwestern college town transported to California. Their faculties are parochial, the administration reactionary, and the students for the most part affluent and careerist.

At the time, I was pleased to leave the stale halls of Harvard for the fragrant spaces of California. I was ready to adopt the way of life of my alter ego, Jean-Jacques Rousseau. I arrived in 1972 and took up residence with a friend in a remote cabin in Bear Canyon located four thousand feet above Claremont in the San Gabriel Mountains.

Within a year I had established a European Studies Program at the Graduate School and had garnered a hefty grant from the National Endowment for the Humanities to underwrite it. Though marketed as an interdisciplinary program, it was in fact based on the work of Foucault and his circle. I was trying to inject into the mainstream of American academe the methods and ideas of the Parisian spokesmen of the "Molecular Revolution," which during the sixties in America was termed "the Movement." I felt that Foucault and Deleuze were not only providing the most advanced thinking for the Molecular Revolution but at the same time were transforming our understanding of the human sciences.

THE FORMULA

When I learned that Foucault would be teaching at Berkeley I jumped at the chance of inviting him to Claremont. What an opportunity, I thought. We could meet the great man face-to-face. The writing would be clarified for us by the very presence of the writer. His visit might even focus world attention on the European Studies Program and thereby help to consolidate our little avant-garde outpost in one of the most reactionary regions of California.

So, the overriding issue for me was how to entice such an acclaimed figure to a college town of no importance. Before trying to sell him on the idea, I made an inventory of things in our favor. I would tell him about the European Studies Program in the hope that our dedication to his work and our involvement in the Movement would persuade him to visit us. I would get him a generous honorarium. I could promise a bevy of California young men to entertain him. I would propose taking him to some scenic California locales.

Then I had a brainstorm. If I was successful in arranging a visit by Michel Foucault, I would conduct an experiment. I concocted a formula that I felt might produce an intellectual power approaching the wonders of science fiction, something on the order of Dr. Morbius in *Forbidden Planet,* or the Galaxy Being from the first episode of *The Outer Limits.*

Here was my formula: first, take the world's greatest intellect, the man who went beyond the nostrum that "knowledge is power" to figure out that "power produces knowledge"; second, provide this intellect with a heavenly elixir, a digestible philosopher's stone, which has the potential of increasing astronomically the power of the brain; enchantment.

I would be the alchemist and document the experiment. The formula read as follows: Michel Foucault + The Philosopher's Stone + Death Valley, California + Michael Stoneman.

MICHAEL STONEMAN is my life partner and, in his words, "a composer, a homosexual, and a smoker." He has many interests, including a predilection for things Chinese, especially their language, their religions, and their magical herbs.

Shortly after we met on Thanksgiving 1974, Michael stated he wished to initiate me into the mystery of things. He took me to Death Valley, which is a magnificent terrain of desert and mountains about two hundred miles from Los Angeles almost to the Nevada border. There I experienced rapture and illumination that I had never dreamed could exist.

Now we had the opportunity to provide the same for Michel Foucault. Like two faces of Eve, we would offer him the fruit from the Tree of Knowledge. We would have a Night on Bald Mountain.

I thought that a Death Valley trip would give Foucault the kind of experience of enlightenment we associate with the luminous teachers of the past. I knew we were taking a risk. Ingesting the philosopher's stone in such an enchanted locale might blow the fuses of the master thinker of our era. Or it might have no effect at all.

Nevertheless, I held fast to the expectation that the event would elicit from Foucault gnomic utterances of such power that he would unleash a veritable revolution in consciousness. Had not Artaud received his tongue of fire after taking peyote trips with the Tarahumara Indians in the Grand Canyon of Mexico? And couldn't we expect more, much more, from Michel Foucault?

As it turned out, my formula might be considered something of a delusion of grandeur. The Death Valley trip did not change the world, but it transformed Michel Foucault, who said it was the greatest experience of his life. When he got back to Paris, he wrote to Mike and me that he had to begin anew. The Death Valley trip had changed him completely. He stated that upon his return he threw the completed second volume of *The History of Sexuality* into the fire and eradicated the entire prospectus of books he had meant to publish in the projected seven-volume series. He planned to start over.

The results of that new beginning can be seen in the last three volumes of *The History of Sexuality,* which were written after the Death Valley trip. They crown his body of work like the *Ethics* caps the corpus of Aristotle. Foucault's final message to us is the supreme value of the "aesthetics of existence." He teaches us to elude the ruinous codes of the Disciplined Society and to make our lives into works of art.

I believe the Death Valley trip was instrumental in making Foucault's *Ethics* possible, as well as determining its substance.

THE VERY AFTERNOON Phyllis Johnson, a French professor at Pomona College, an ally in the European Studies Program, and a very dear friend, told me that Foucault was coming to California, I placed a call to the chairman of the French department at Berkeley. He assured me that Foucault had accepted the appointment at Berkeley, but the department had yet to learn when he would arrive, what he would teach, or whether he would be available for any public lectures at Berkeley or anywhere else. He suggested that I write directly to Foucault in Paris. To my surprise he gave me Foucault's home address, which I pinned above my desk as a medieval monk might have incised the route to Rome on the wall of his cell.

I sent a note to Foucault in Paris, inviting him to Claremont. He replied succinctly that he would very much like to visit us but that since he did not know his schedule or his responsibilities at Berkeley he would have to wait until his arrival in California before making any travel plans. He requested that I write to him at Berkeley.

I wrote and suggested a trip to Death Valley, which I described with a line from Artaud's account of his peyote experience with the Tarahumara Indians: "suspended among the forms hoping for nothing but the wind." The letter also provided prolix details of a projected schedule of seminars, lectures, and parties. Looking back on the demanding program I foolishly proposed, it is not surprising Foucault did not answer. I was crestfallen.

IRVINE

In early May, I heard again from Phyllis Johnson that Foucault was to give a lecture at the University of California in Irvine, about an hour's drive from Claremont. The news immediately set my pulse racing. I would confront him face-to-face. I knew the importance of being earnest. Michael and my two student allies, Brit and Patti, met me at the auditorium hoping to catch a glimpse of Foucault when he entered the hall. Brit grabbed me by the arm and gasped, "There he is!"

And there he was, striding vigorously toward the entrance. He was considerably shorter and more compact than I had imagined him from the severe, unsmiling photograph on the jacket of *The Order of Things*. He had broad shoulders and a round face, definitely Frankish, with features more pleasantly modulated and animated than in the picture.

For a moment I thought we were mistaken, but in the next instant I made a few quick steps, leaps really, to get a better look at him. "Yes, it is Foucault," I said to Patti, who was right behind me. His eyes possessed the laserbeam intensity evident in the photograph, and the bald-eagle cranium was unmistakable. Upon closer look the bare skull was marked by several extra lobes, which bulged from the apex of the brain stem. One did not have to be a phrenologist to recognize that an extraordinary cerebral mutation, something on the order of a supermind, had emerged from the outer limits.

Foucault's white turtleneck under an open madras jacket revealed a powerful torso with well-defined contours. His white bell-bottom trousers fit him closely around the pelvis and thighs. He looked like an athlete rather than an academic. Obviously he did not spend all his time crouched over a desk.

We followed him into the hall and took seats in the second row in front of the lectern. As the audience filed in, Foucault sat easy and alert, referring to his notes and conferring with the moderator, with whom he laughed from time to time in response to some observation inaudible to us. Occasionally he would look around and study the faces of the assembled group.

After a brief introduction, which consisted of the words "Michel Foucault" followed by warm applause, the distinguished visitor from Paris stepped with alacrity to the lectern. I had heard that Foucault adamantly refused to lecture in English and so I was not surprised to find him reading his notes in French.

His lecture on the proliferation of sexual discourse during the nineteenth century was clearly part of the renowned course he had offered that year at the Collège de France. He placed his focus on the pervasive and obsessive condemnation of masturbation in medical and religious literature. Most likely the lecture was taken from the then completed manuscript of the second volume of *The History of Sexuality,* the same manuscript he was to destroy upon returning to Paris after the Death Valley trip.

The moderator informed the audience that Foucault had just a little time before catching a plane back to San Francisco and so he would have to limit the discussion period to a few questions. After a brief interchange with the audience, Foucault walked quickly toward the exit.

I could not muster the courage to break through the entourage that accompanied him as he was shuffled out the door. I was devastated, since I felt that this might be my last chance to invite him to take a trip with us. Suddenly, with amazing celerity, Michael darted toward Foucault, negotiated through the crowd of admirers engulfing him, and stated in breathless French that I wished to speak with him. Baffled by Michael's brazen entreaty, and puzzled by a name that he did not immediately recognize, Foucault stood still long enough for me to reach him.

I was so surprised by Michael's adroitness in cornering Foucault that all I could do was utter my name and Claremont, two words I repeated three times. Then Foucault, overlooking my gaucheness, remembered my letter and at once apologized for not having replied. "I fear I have been rude," he stated in clear English. "But I have so many engagements while I am in California that I do not think I will have time to visit Claremont on this trip." Then his hosts edged him toward the door, but I held my position by his side, stumbling clumsily most of the way up the stairs while attempting to persuade him to come see us if only for a day.

At last we reached the top of the stairs and the open air. Foucault stopped suddenly, turned toward me with a smile, and said, "But how can I see the Valley of Death if I only spend one day with you?"

My hopes rose along with renewed powers of speech. "Then come down for three or four days," I proposed. "We could drive to Death Valley, spend the night and the following morning, then drive back in the afternoon in time for you to give a talk in Claremont. It only takes a little over four hours to get to Death Valley from Claremont," I added with an imploring smile.

"We shall see," he said. "Call me at my office in Berkeley tomorrow afternoon."

But he could not get away fast enough to avoid Michael, who rushed toward him with Hitchcockian abruptness and asked if he practiced hatha yoga. Startled, Foucault replied with a "What?," then a "No."

"I thought you might do yoga since you have such a beautiful body," Michael shouted as Foucault's hosts disengaged him from the circle of well-wishers and hustled him toward their car. One could easily have supposed that a politician was leaving a rally under the protection of the secret service.

The following week I phoned Foucault in Berkeley. "I have decided to visit you in Claremont," he said emphatically. "I hope we will have time to visit the Valley of Death."

Trembling with anticipation I assured him we would most assuredly take a trip to Death Valley. Then I gave him a brief sketch of our plans.

"Just as long as I don't have to speak to a large group of people. I have had enough of that."

"I hope not. Will you speak in English?"

"I would rather not. My English is so bad."

"Can you arrive on Friday? Perhaps we can make it to Joshua Tree National Park as well."

"Out of the question. No sooner than Saturday."

"Then we will pick you up at the airport. We will spend Memorial Day weekend in Death Valley. Send me the time of your arrival. Are you sure you will recognize us?"

"Well, in any case you will certainly not fail to recognize me," Foucault, alluding most likely to his bald head, said with a laugh.

ARRIVAL

After going to ridiculous lengths of preparation, my "this must be a dream" day arrived. On the way to the airport, Michael listened sympathetically to my exclamations about the privilege of receiving such a visit and about my feelings of inadequacy in the face of it. For such a momentous event, one would have thought that I would have remembered the exact time of his arrival. Fortunately the plane was late, and as the electric-eye doors swung open we encountered Foucault striding toward the baggage room as if the airport were on fire.

"Monsieur Foucault!" I exclaimed. "We have found you!"

"Yes," he smiled back broadly after twisting around like a contortionist, "and I am very happy to see you and Michael."

Except for the copy of the *LA Times* clutched in his hand, Foucault appeared just as he had at Irvine. The whole ensemble was the same—brown madras jacket, white turtleneck sweater, white tapered trousers, brown loafers. After getting his small valise and a box of papers, we boarded our green Volvo sedan and made for the freeway. I asked him why he had brought all those papers and he said they were notes for a book he was writing on man and monster. He was also giving a seminar on the subject at Berkeley.

We could have been almost anywhere on the California freeway system as the cool fog dimmed the streams of light along Route 10. Michael asked Foucault if this was his first trip to California. I knew he had lived and taught all over the world—Stockholm, Istanbul, Tunis, Brazil, Lisbon, Hanover, Clermont-Ferrand, Buffalo. Consequently, I was surprised to learn that he had never been to California before his present teaching sojourn at Berkeley.

"I have wanted to visit California for a long time now," Foucault told us. "I prefer hot climates and I have spent a lot of time in North Africa. I do not like living in Paris. It is too cold and cramped and the Parisians are stuffy. The boys are vain."

"Yes," I said, "a flock of peacocks. Why do you stay there?"

"Love and work," he replied. "My lover lives there and my job is not very demanding. I only have to lecture once a week for three months out of the year. Right now it would be difficult to match that anywhere else."

Michael asked him how he liked San Francisco. Foucault replied that he was enjoying the city very much. He told us that he had subletted a student's room in Berkeley at first but, finding that the university town curled up at dusk, he had moved across the bay to a rooming house not far from Folsom Street, which at the time was a center of the gay leather scene.

I told Foucault that Michael was a linguist, who up to then had mastered ten languages and their subtongues. He and Mike then began to speak in French. My understanding of spoken French being poor compelled me to tell Foucault that Mike was also a pianist and composer.

Foucault leaned forward from the back seat, where he had insisted upon sitting, and responded with animated delight.

"Wonderful," he said to Michael. "I love music and hope that I can hear something of yours. Do you know the music of Pierre Boulez? He is a great friend of mine."

"Oh really," we said in unison. I referred to an excellent *New Yorker* profile of Boulez by Peter Heyworth, the music critic for the *London Observer*. Foucault had not read it, so I told him that Heyworth described Boulez's compositions as the greatest revolution in twentieth-century music. I added that Stockhausen once stated that Boulez was the only composer he could talk to.

"I have known Boulez for a long time now," Foucault said, "and recently I have made arrangements for him to teach at the Collège de France. Not right in the Collège de France, but at the new Institut pour la Recherche de la Musique Moderne just outside Paris. This deal has taken some doing, for it will be the first time a professor at the Collège de France will be allowed to teach outside its walls. But the director of the Collège agreed to the idea, and Boulez was anxious to give up conducting and return to Paris and to teaching. I think this will be a very satisfactory arrangement."

"Do you listen to music very much, Michel?" Michael asked.

"There was a long time when I did not listen to music," Michel lamented. "But I have come to recognize the importance of music again and am able to listen closely to it. In fact, I've done almost nothing else for the last three years."

"What kind of music? Classical? Modern?"

"Yes!" he said.

"Do you listen to pop and rock music?" Michael continued.

"No. But I will say this: It certainly has a lot of influence on people all over the world, especially the lyrics," Foucault remarked. Mike stated that he didn't have enough time to listen to all the worthwhile classical music, so he couldn't spend time on pop music. I chimed in that pop music was good for dancing, but otherwise monotonous. "And the beat goes on," I concluded.

As we rode along we drafted our plans for the next few days. The only suggestion Foucault did not take to was a swing around West Hollywood nightlife. He told us that he had had enough of that in San Francisco. We turned off the freeway and in a few minutes arrived at our airplane bungalow house, which hovered above Route 66 like an irradiated riverboat floating on a cloud of mist. To our right the rugged mountains of the San Gabriel range were obscured, and the wide expanse of chaparral stretching from the house to the foothills of Mount Baldy was enshrouded in fog.

CHEZ FOUCAULT

"*Oh là là,*" Foucault exclaimed as he entered the house. "*Très beau; merveilleuse!*" he said as he took a sweeping glance of Mike's paintings and my photography on the walls. From the back, our dog rushed out of the kitchen to greet him. "I love dogs," he said, dissuading me from pulling her away from him. He scratched her belly, which she always presented to her admirers, and absorbed the ambience of the large living room.

"Skadi is a Norwegian Elkhound," I volunteered. "Do you have a dog?"

"No, it is so difficult to keep a dog in Paris, but my mother has one at her place in the country, so I get to enjoy it there."

"Let me take your things into the waterbed room," Mike offered.

"Just show me where you would like me to put them," Foucault insisted. "I can manage."

"Have you ever slept on a waterbed?" Mike queried.

"Never have."

"Then you must try this one while you are here," I offered. "It even has a vibrator under the mattress. It doesn't take long to become a sybarite in Southern California."

"But we don't just cavort on the waterbed," Mike pointed out. "We practice yoga too."

I reminded Foucault that Mike had asked him about yoga at Irvine.

"Ah, yes. That was Michael, wasn't it? I was so rushed. The whole incident is a haze."

"If you do not do yoga, how do you stay in such good shape?" Mike asked.

"I do gymnastics," Foucault replied.

"We would like to teach you yoga while you are here," I told him.

"I would like that very much," he said.

I produced a book of hatha yoga photographs. Foucault went through it assiduously and, pointing to a most difficult position of standing on one's hands with legs over the head, devilishly asked, with a broad smile displaying his large white teeth, "Can you do that?"

"Not yet," I answered meekly. "But I intend to."

"I noticed the *Tao Te Ching* on a table in the living room," Foucault continued. "Are you interested in Taoism?"

"Yes, for a few years now," I answered. "It is the philosophy of life that I try to follow. After all, doesn't 'the way' of the *Tao Te Ching* amount to the same as the cultivation of ch'i energy—what Wilhelm Reich called 'orgone'? Have you studied Reich, Michel? Have you read the late works, such as *The Cancer Biopathy*?"

"I have not spent much time with Reich," he responded sternly. "I believe I have only read one book by him."

"I hope you will read *Cosmic Superimposition*," I said, feeling slightly silly for telling Michel Foucault what he should read. "I am convinced by Reich's experiments. I can feel the streaming of orgone when I am doing yoga or having sex. Are they doing yoga and reading Lao Tzu in France?" I inquired.

"Neither! Europe is far behind California. It appears to me that California has severed itself from the mainland and is drifting toward Asia. Having visited California I now understand why people who live here when they travel abroad say they are from California rather than from America. No one who lives in Pennsylvania would say, 'I am from Pennsylvania.' California and America are not the same."

"This is true," I said. "Until I came to California I lived in the South and the East. These are regions tied to class and tradition. But here in Southern California I am amazed at how people, especially the young people like Michael and his friends, live without history, almost without family, at least in the traditional sense, deterritorialized in the Deleuzian sense, but maintaining a deep reverence for the surrounding mountains, ocean, and desert."

"Yes," Foucault said smiling. "It's wonderful, isn't it? Do you think you would ever move back East?"

"Frankly, no."

"Others have told me the same thing. Leo Bersani, my colleague at Berkeley, said he wouldn't, he really couldn't leave California."

On the way to join Michael in the kitchen Foucault lingered in the dining room to examine the herbarium. For the moment he showed no further interest in the books or artwork that I had so carefully displayed to catch his eye.

WHILE FOUCAULT SAT quietly in the living room, Mike and I served up a small meal.

"Have you ever had a Tequila Sunrise?" Michael inquired.

"No, but I would like to try one," Foucault responded.

"It is very strong," Mike cautioned.

"I am used to strong drinks," Foucault declared with a complicitous grin. "In North Africa there are very potent drinks, but I must confess that my favorite is a Bloody Mary. Would you show me how to make a Tequila Sunrise?" Foucault asked as he walked into the kitchen. While the two of them concocted the brew, I began to transport the snacks into the living room. Again, Foucault, who always resisted being waited on, insisted upon helping.

"The Tequila Sunrise is delicious, rather exotic, and the salt is a great idea," Foucault said before he took a second sip of his drink, the last sip. He took a few bites of Boursin and a few slices of sausage deftly speared and consumed with relish, but no more. He always ate sparingly.

"Would you care to smoke some marijuana? One of Simeon's students gave us a joint, which you are welcome to," Mike added.

"Yes, I would like a joint," Foucault affirmed.

"Have you ever smoked grass before?" I inquired.

"I have been smoking it for years, particularly when I was in North Africa, where they have marvelous hashish."

"And do you smoke grass in Paris?" I persisted.

"Grass is very hard to come by in Paris, but I smoke hash whenever I can get a hold of some. We have been in good supply recently, thanks to Noam Chomsky."

"How did that happen?" I asked.

"I appeared with Chomsky on TV in Amsterdam, and after the show the sponsors of the program asked me what kind of remuneration I would like. I told them that I would like some hashish, and happily they complied with my wish with a large block of the stuff. My students and I refer to it as the Chomsky hash, not because Chomsky himself had anything to do with it but because he occasioned it."

"What was your impression of Chomsky?" I asked.

"A very agreeable man. We did not have much time to talk. And the moderator did a very stupid thing. He wanted us to have a debate. So he described Chomsky as an American liberal, even an anarchist, and me as a Marxist. It was absurd. I am not a Marxist, and such labels are ridiculous, particularly applied to Chomsky and me. Actually, we just had a pleasant discussion."

"I met Chomsky once," I said, "when he spoke to a small group of us at Dunster House at Harvard during the antiwar years in the sixties. I found him incredibly honest, so intense and incisive when he talked about the folly of destroying a country under the pretense of saving it. Don't you think that Chomsky has effected a veritable revolution in our understanding of language?"

"Definitely. What he has given us really is a theory of communication. That's where his achievement lies. His interest is in communication."

"And the Chomsky hash, did you have any trouble getting it into France?"

"No, not really."

"So you smoke it with your students?"

"Yes. Often after my lecture we go someplace where we smoke hash and laugh a lot."

"Have you ever heard any music by Jean Barraqué?" Foucault, changing the subject, asked Michael.

"No, but I do know he is an important French composer," Mike responded.

"I arranged some poems by Nietzsche for Barraqué and he used them for a song cycle called *Séquence*. I believe the cycle is dated 1955, but they were begun in 1950."

"I can check that," Mike offered.

He returned with a copy of H. H. Stuckenschmidt's *Twentieth Century Music*. "You are right, *Séquence* is dated 1950."

"Barraqué and I lived together in Paris for three years," Foucault said. "They were marvelous years and our parting was difficult for me. I dropped everything and went to Sweden."

"Why did you split up?" I asked.

"Alcoholism," Foucault responded. "He couldn't give it up. I suppose that is a major reason why the work of Malcolm Lowry magnetizes me. He is the greatest. There are two ways to go: with Lowry into intoxication and the other way. Neither is necessarily better than the other."

"When did you part?" I inquired, with unrelenting persistence.

"In 1956."

"That would have been only a couple of years after the publication of your first book, a translation with an introduction to Binswanger's *Dream and Existence*. I ran across it at the Bibliotheque Nationale a couple of summers ago."

"I thought I had seen you somewhere before!" Foucault exclaimed. "I must have spotted you there while you were reading that summer. I am sure of it."

"Certainly possible, though I would not remember since I had my head in a book the whole time. Your books, probably," I said with a laugh. "How strange to think that I could have met you then. At any rate, I was really impressed with the correlation you drew in your treatise on dreams between literary genres and dream analysis. I am puzzled that you did not mention it again in your subsequent work."

"I don't know why I did not develop that notion," Foucault responded. "I do not even remember it."

"There are so many provocative ideas in your early works that you never followed up. For instance, the arresting paragraph on madness and the collective unconscious in *Madness and Civilization*. You observe that we can perceive the entire history of madness in the bodily movements of individuals confined in psychiatric hospitals. That passage did not even make it into the English edition."

"Is that true? I suspect you know more about my writings than I do," Foucault declared with a smile.

"I certainly am impressed with the English translators of your works, particularly A. M. Sheridan Smith. What do you think of the translations of your books?" I asked.

Foucault squirmed impatiently and then responded, "I have no thoughts on the subject. I have never read my books!"

"When do you do your writing?" Mike inquired.

"In the morning," Foucault answered. "I work about five hours a day and leave the rest of my time for other things."

AFTER A WHILE I suggested to Foucault that he might like to hear Michael play the piano. Foucault welcomed the idea enthusiastically.

Michael sat down at the Yamaha grand and gave us a spirited reading of Scriabin's Tenth Sonata, a work of pure sorcery. As soon as he had finished playing, Foucault, who had listened attentively, was demonstrative in his expression of gratitude.

"Very, very beautiful," he declared. "It takes me back to the night I met Boulez. It was at a Scriabin recital in Paris. We were both students at the time, and I spotted him alone at the back of the hall. I asked my companion if he knew the attractive young man and he did. We were introduced, and from that time we have seen each other frequently."

While Foucault and Michael continued their conversation about Boulez and contemporary music, I brought in some coffee and prepared the pipe for a round of tokes. As I handed the pipe to Foucault I asked him if he knew the Don Juan books by Carlos Castaneda, the UCLA anthropology professor who had startled academia with his story about a shaman who used marijuana and peyote in his visionary quests.

"I have read only the first, but frankly I do not remember very much about it," he replied.

"Another book out of Mexico which interests me is Ivan Illich's

Deschooling Society. Do you know it?" I inquired.

"Yes, and I too have a high opinion of the thesis of the book. Illich is a man with one good idea. I see you have here Deleuze's *Proust and Signs.* What do you think of it?"

"I consider it the best book about Proust I have ever read."

"I agree totally; it is the best," Foucault observed.

"Have you read Proust recently?" I asked.

"Yes, quite by accident," he replied. "The student's room I stayed in when I first arrived in Berkeley had a copy of *Le Temps retrouvé.* I happened upon it and read it through."

"Any new impressions?" I asked.

"It is a very intelligent book," he replied.

After his gaze meandered over the large coffee table crammed with books I had set out to capture his attention, Foucault picked up a copy of R. D. Laing's *Knots.* "I really like this one," he stated, as if he knew that I had put out some bait to catch his eye and spark some conversation. "It is Laing's best—his best *theoretical* book," Foucault said, emphasizing the word "theoretical."

"Do you continue to read works about madness and civilization—Erving Goffman, Ken Kesey, that renegade Szasz, for example?" I asked.

Foucault responded, "I have recently read a very interesting book by an Italian on the relationships between the asylum and political power."

I told Foucault that *Madness and Civilization* made a great impact upon me. "It changed my life," I said. "But it took so long to make an impact in this country."

"As a matter of fact," Foucault said, "I sent the manuscript to five different publishers in Paris before I could find one to print it. And even then I only got it published because a friend of mine championed it before the board of editors of Pion, who published it but did not bother to read it. All the other publishers claimed it was an insane book—unintelligible, verbose, and unsalable. I have only received a few thousand dollars from royalties. The contract was not exactly equitable. But it is a very old book now."

Mike was getting fidgety. He edged toward the tape deck and I was reminded of Foucault's request in the car to hear some of Mike's music. With Foucault's consent we listened to *Homage to Mizoguchi*, a fantasia of electronic sounds, wind chimes, and Japanese words spoken by Michael and modulated mechanically to produce strange echoes and overlapping. Mizoguchi's film *Sansho the Bailiff* had occasioned the work. The composition included voices from a Japanese soap opera and concluded with a group of Japanese men singing in English "You Are My Sunshine." This made Foucault laugh.

"It is like a Noh drama," Foucault said. "It captures the essence of the Noh play. I like it very much. Have you ever been to Japan, Michael?"

"No, but I sure would like to."

"It is strange to be in a place where you cannot even read the direction signs. Very disorienting all round. How about Paris? Have you been there?"

"No," Mike responded.

"Well, I would like to make arrangements for you to study with

Boulez in Paris. Are you interested?"

"Sure. But I will need to confer with Simeon. Maybe we both can come to Paris."

"You and Simeon are welcome to stay with me anytime."

So honored was I to receive such an invitation that I proclaimed to Foucault that I considered myself one of his disciples, though I knew he probably disliked the term. I guess my Southern Baptist upbringing sometimes still had its effect on my speech. Without answering, Foucault just gazed at me with steely-eyed intentness.

DEATH VALLEY TRIP

We took breakfast at dawn and then cautiously negotiated through the smog-laden streets of Claremont. I mentioned that some of the natives, presumably protecting their property values, call the smog "haze" on the grounds that the original Indian inhabitants referred to the region as "hazy valley." I pointed out that during the summer and fall the smog is so thick in this region of Southern California that the mayor of Riverside, a nearby town, had suggested building huge fans to blow it back into the city.

"We try to escape the smog as much as possible by getting to the mountains or out into the desert," Mike said, "far away from the scurry and strife of humankind."

"We have prepared something special for you to take in the desert," I interjected.

"What's that?" Foucault asked wide-eyed.

"We brought along a powerful elixir, a kind of philosopher's stone Michael happened upon. We thought you might enjoy a visionary quest in Death Valley."

The landscape alone is liable to have something of a magical effect upon you. It is a kind of Shangri-la, protected from microwave radiation and other forms of pollution.

"I would like that," Foucault responded without the slightest hesitation. "I can hardly wait to get started."

Mike and I smiled mischievously at each other as I accelerated on the entrance ramp to Route 10, which would carry us to San Bernardino, where we joined the highway to what Foucault called "the Valley of Death."

"Do you go to films and the theater?" I asked Foucault.

"The theater, never. I have completely lost interest in the theater, but I do like films a lot. Actually, I am presently involved in making a film based on a recent book I edited called *Pierre Rivière*."

"I have read your book. I was particularly impressed with the boy's 'Autobiography' and your essay on the canard. I did not much care for the other essays by your students."

"Neither did I."

"Are you writing a filmscript?"

"Yes. But recently I have been working with the director to find a boy without any acting experience to play the leading role, someone fresh from the country."

"Like Louis Malle's *Lacombe, Lucien*?"

"Yes, exactly. We have found the right boy and I am very happy with our choice. We expect the preparations for the film to take considerable time, but I am enjoying the work immensely."

"Other than Antonioni I guess my favorite contemporary filmmaker is Jean-Luc Godard. Do you happen to know him?"

"Yes, I do. You know he changed very much after his motorcycle accident. He has become bitter and difficult. I just happened to be in my car right behind Godard when it happened. He was crushed between two cars and one whole side of his body was flayed."

"Doubly ironic after *Weekend,* which I guess was partly occasioned by his special horror of automobiles. According to one account I read, both his mother and his first wife were killed in car accidents."

"I did not know that."

"Once I met Godard, in Claremont of all places," I went on to say. "I told him how much I admired *Le Mépris* with Brigitte Bardot and Jack Palance. 'I don't like it one bit' were the words Godard hurled into my face. 'It's not political enough,' he said. Godard informed me that he was not a Marxist when he made that film, but that at least he could detect his imminent conversion to Marxism in the film."

"Godard is a political bitch!" Foucault interjected sharply.

"And rude," I added. "When he was leaving the dinner, Godard confronted the host with, 'Why do you Americans always shake hands? Why don't you try something else, like grabbing my thigh or spitting?' Frankly, I did not consider Godard's thigh enticing enough to grab."

We passed through the town of Chino. I told Foucault about the minimum-security prison there, a so-called model prison.

"I am aware of your focus on the function of prisons in our society," I said to Foucault. "Did you not create a mechanism whereby French prisoners could correspond with each other and write about their lives and their grievances? A Parisian friend told me a few years ago that your efforts on behalf of French prisoners had made you a celebrity with the general public, that you had even been featured in women's magazines on that account."

"I do not know about the women's magazines," Foucault said, "but sometimes I feel like a vedette. At any rate, I was involved in the Groupe d'information sur les prisons, which was not reformist in the sense that we had any notion of an ideal prison, but we wished to facilitate means to allow the prisoners to speak for themselves about what is intolerable in the system. We did create a newsletter, which was written and edited by prisoners, but we had great difficulties in getting it published and it no longer exists."

"I understand you wrote something about your impressions of Attica, which you visited after the uprising and massacre of the prisoners there, and in the article you said that the American prison is different from the French."

"As a matter of fact," Foucault said, "I have never been inside a French prison. The authorities would never allow it. Have you read *Soledad Brother*, the prison letters of George Jackson? I have been very moved by them. Genet, Deleuze, and I recently collaborated on an introduction to a French edition of the letters."

I confessed that I had not read the letters but had recently run across Genet's *May Day Speech* when I was browsing in the City Lights bookstore in San Francisco. "Genet certainly made a powerful statement on behalf of the Black Panthers," I said.

"Genet has been very interested in the Black Panthers," Foucault continued. "A strange thing happened shortly after we published Jackson's letters. Genet learned that the murder of Jackson was an inside job; he was the casualty of a feud in his own group."

"Do you see Genet and Deleuze often?" I asked.

"Yes, I do. Genet and I are very close. You know he is so elusive. Wherever he lives he always stays adjacent to a railway station with bags packed. He says it's habit. He has to feel he can get away fast. Once, I was walking near the Palais-Royal with Genet and Deleuze. A lady approached us suddenly and said, pointing to him, 'Aren't you Jean Genet?' Genet turned to us and said with exasperation, 'Why do they always recognize *me*?'"

"I am curious what Genet thought of Sartre's biography of him," Michael inquired after we had finished our good laugh over the preceding anecdote.

"Genet said it was a great book," Foucault answered with a flash of his white teeth, which looked like they had all been crowned, "only that Sartre didn't understand *anything* about him, not the first thing."

This observation started another round of laughter.

"Having read Deleuze and Guattari's revolutionary book on capitalism and schizophrenia," I continued, "I have wondered if Deleuze is a kind of 'off-the-wall' person."

"Actually, Deleuze wouldn't strike you as being all that unusual," Foucault replied. "He appears completely conventional. He is married and has two children."

"How did Deleuze and Guattari meet?"

"Through his philosophical studies Deleuze became interested in schizophrenia. He looked around Paris to find someone to tell him more about schizophrenia. A friend suggested Guattari, who at the time was running a retreat for mentally ill people in the South of France."

MICHAEL SERVED UP some hot Irish coffee from the Japanese airport.

"I am very surprised that you have never experimented with psychedelics," Mike said to Foucault. "Aren't the best kinds available to you in Europe? After all, LSD was discovered by Albert Hofmann in Switzerland just a few weeks after the atom bomb was invented. A momentous conjuncture."

"I have had the opportunity, but have never taken it," Foucault rejoined. "My lover always refused, and I abided by his wishes."

"I would have thought," I interposed, "that R. D. Laing would have encouraged you to experience altered states. But then, that assumes you and Laing are friends. At least I presume you know each other, since some of your books were published in English under the imprint of Laing's World of Man series."

"No. In fact, I have never met Laing. It was David Cooper, Laing's friend and colleague, who negotiated the publishing arrangement for the English translations."

"How did Cooper come to know about *Madness and Civilization*?"

"Both Cooper and Laing were very much affected by the writings of Sartre. Cooper continued to read extensively in French writings on philosophy and psychology. He just happened upon my book in Paris and subsequently asked me if he could publish the work in English. I consented, and that was the beginning of our friendship."

"Do you still see Cooper?"

"Cooper lives in Paris now and he came by for dinner shortly after arriving. He was an unhappy man, completely at loose ends. He no longer works with Laing. He gave a lecture in Paris not so long ago, and though I did not attend the lecture, I understand that he lamented that Laing had reverted to classical theories of psychology and had abandoned the work they were doing together."

"I really like the title they gave to the English edition of *Les mots et les choses*. But why did you change it?"

"There were already a few books of note in English with the title *Words and Things*. As a matter of fact, I much prefer the title *The Order of Things*. I really wanted the original French edition to bear that title, but it was thought that *L'Ordre des choses* would sound like a biology book about the classification of species."

We gazed at the impressive four-tiered freeway interchange straight ahead in the distance. Foucault commented on the ferocity of the smog and told us that he thought l'air Paris was bad but it was nothing compared to this.

AFTER A SHORT INTERVAL of silence I asked Foucault if he had liked his year of teaching at Vincennes, which I knew purported at the time to be a radical outpost of the University of Paris.

"I detested it," he said. "The whole structure—grading students, etc.—was tedious, a nuisance. There were so many girls. I loathed reading all the little essays, a particular academic ritual I cannot bear.

I was very happy to get out of there."

I expressed my own frustration about the traditional educational format. I told Foucault how compromised I felt working in a cluster of colleges dominated by a Reaganoid mentality and a sickening religiosity. I explained that I even felt guilty about getting federal funding for my European Studies Program under the present administration.

"I understand your feelings very well," he said. "As well as your submission to the financial realities of education in our society. I have been sharply criticized by French leftists for teaching at the state-supported Collège de France and working to get money and jobs for students. But what else can we do? Students have to make a living."

"Do you vote, Michel?"

"Yes, I do, and I have been criticized from the left for that too. I voted for Mitterrand, and some leftists said why waste your time in electoral politics, we need a revolution. I say this to them: Are you really sure you want a revolution?"

"I understand what you are saying. Are you not amazed at how much all the heads of state and the bureaucracies in Western countries resemble each other. Isn't it depressing?"

"Yes, I have noticed the likeness."

"I have been teaching my brother, David, who is an attorney, about your work. I am counting on him and all the other students of your way of thinking to reform our institutions," I said.

"Reform?" Foucault blurted out forcefully. His intonation was filled with such contempt that I was stunned. Later Foucault sent me his own personal copy of *Surveiller et punir*, which I framed in a kind of little prison, much to his amusement. It was only then that I learned how the Disciplined Society—Foucault's term for modern Western civilization—continually renews itself by "reform." In the late eighteenth century, the Disciplined Society was born in the bad faith of reform. Under the guise of reforming the prison, it really instituted a new kind of prison far more cruel and counterproductive than anything that had preceded it.

I was being a chatterbox. I brought my questioning to a merciful halt with a reference to Heidegger's phrase "the discipline of keeping silence." Foucault recognized the phrase and appeared visibly relieved when I invoked it. With my expression and tone of voice I implied that I would try to abide by the discipline even though it was difficult for me to keep silent in his presence. There was so much I wanted to know from him and about him.

IT DID NOT TAKE very long for me to transgress our understanding. "Do you remember your dreams, Michel?" I inquired, hoping to get him to speak about his book on the interpretations of dreams.

"No, I cannot," he sighed. "I try to remember them, but after I am awake for a few minutes they just slip my mind. Do you remember yours, Simeon?"

"Oh yes, almost too vividly. Lately I have been dreaming about the leather scene in San Francisco."

"I bet you have," he remarked in a strange tone, as if to say it would be better doing the scene than dreaming about it.

After riding quietly through the desiccated mountains for about fifteen minutes, once again I broke the discipline and blurted out, "Michel, do you have much to do with Lévi-Strauss at the Collège de France? I was outraged when he canceled his seminar after his students objected to his joining the Académie française. When I read his pompous speech to the academy about the necessity of traditional institutions, I was even more put off."

"Lévi-Strauss is a very conservative man," Foucault avowed. "And sometimes he behaves very badly. He writes too many books, which keeps him enclosed in his study. Consequently, he doesn't know the world. Scholars make a great mistake in endeavoring to write and publish all they have to say. We should write only a few good books and leave it to our students to complete the tasks we have begun. Otherwise the scholar spends too little time in the world and does not get to know the world."

"Has Lévi-Strauss read your work?"

"I guess so. He once said to me that for the life of him he could not figure out what I was doing. He claimed to be completely mystified by my books."

"I have been mystified by one thing you wrote. It was a piece you did for *Tel Quel* on Robbe-Grillet and the new French novel. I found it almost perfunctory."

"Frankly, I agree with you. In a sense it *was* perfunctory. I wrote the piece in the early sixties when *Tel Quel* and the experimental novel needed support. I submitted the essay as a favor for the *Tel*

Quel group, a sign of solidarity with their effort to create new styles and forms. But Philippe Sollers and his circle *think* they are going to change the world with books!" Foucault resoundingly concluded.

"Are there any novelists that have made a great impact upon you?" I asked.

"Malcolm Lowry," Foucault gave back quickly. "*Under the Volcano.* Faulkner too, and Thomas Mann had a great influence upon me when I was a student in Paris. But Faulkner is the most important. A few years ago my lover and I took a trip through Faulkner country. We started in New Orleans and traveled through Creole country to the antebellum regions of Mississippi. We only got as far as Natchez. We intended to reach Oxford, Faulkner's home, but it was too far and we had run out of time."

"Strange, you never mention these figures in your work."

"I never mention the people who have made the greatest impact on me," Foucault said wryly. "Do you know a novel by Jean-Antoine ———?" I don't remember the full name Foucault gave me and was always too embarrassed to admit it when I saw him again.

"No."

"It is a marvelous autobiographical novel by a young man in his twenties. He started it when he was sixteen and worked steadily in isolation for five years. One Christmas Day a few years ago my lover and I were watching TV when the phone rang and an unfamiliar voice asked me if I would read a new novel. I invited the author over to the flat that afternoon and we became friends. I made arrangements to have the work published."

OUR CONVERSATION WAS abruptly halted by the sight of enormous boulders massed in formation like icebergs crushed against an island. The sharp, traversing planes reminded me of Caspar David Friedrich's *Arctic Shipwreck*. Foucault took note of my comparison. The mountains in the west tilted their quilted flanks toward the morning sun.

Mike awoke from his nap and started a second round of coffee and pipe.

"Have you visited the raunchy Folsom Street bars since you have been in San Francisco?" Michael asked Michel.

"Of course," replied Michel with a jack-o'-lantern grin.

"Even the Barracks?" Michael threw back.

"Yes. What a tough place! Never have I seen such an open display of sexuality in a public bar."

"Do you have the leather man's paraphernalia—leather cap with visor, chaps, tit clamps, and the like?" Mike inquired.

"Oh, absolutely," Foucault responded with a complicitous grin.

"And what about Cabaret?" I interjected, referring to one of the flashy gay dance bars in North Beach.

"I went there just for a few hours one night. So many beautiful young men sporting about with such abandon and joy. There is nothing in France to compare to it. There are not even places where gay people can congregate and dance together in public. In France the bar scene is still furtive and uninviting. Anyway, the bar scene can be too much like prison for gay people. Too forced and anonymous, too confining."

"And what about the baths in San Francisco?" Mike continued.

"Yes, I have been to the baths. One night at the baths I met an attractive young man who told me that he and many others go to the baths a few times a week, frequently under the influence of uppers and amyl. Such a way of life is extraordinary to me, unbelievable. These men live for casual sex and drugs. Incredible! There are no such places in France."

"Simeon and I met at the baths," Mike told Foucault. We all laughed at the preposterousness of it. "The Third Street Athletic Club," Mike added. "We talked for hours in one of the dark cubicles and had sex before we ever saw each other. We were in a bunk room and we broke the taboo against speaking. Adding insult to injury, we talked about music. Chopin and Rachmaninoff, Pollini and Michelangeli. Simeon is a pianist too, you know. We couldn't help ourselves. Eventually everyone else in the room crawled out of their dark corners and departed with a huff."

"Marvelous," Michel interposed with hearty laughter. "When did this happen?"

"A few days before last Thanksgiving," Mike informed him. "Gobble, gobble, gobble!" he warbled while we laughed again.

"I have wondered about something since hearing your lecture about masturbation at Irvine," Mike went on to say. "Do you masturbate?"

"Of course, Michael," Foucault said without hesitation.

"Probably not as much as Simeon likes to," Mike added.

"You are one to talk," I rejoined.

"Do you think we are enjoying our cocks too much?" Mike asked plaintively.

"It's all right if you have the time," Foucault stated sternly, and then he laughed as if we were little boys playing doctor in the back seat of the car. The desert light became intense, so I gave him a pair of reflector sunglasses with broad white rims. I told him that made him look like the child of Kojak and Elton John. He was delighted.

I asked Michel if he was related to the Foucault cited by Freud in his bibliography in *The Interpretation of Dreams*, or to the Foucault who perfected the pendulum.

"No," he replied. "I hated my father. He was a doctor, but unrelated to the person mentioned by Freud. Foucault is a common French name, like Smith in the States."

"What were you like as a boy, Michel? Were you precocious, spending a lot of time studying, impressing your teachers?"

"Hardly. I spent most of my time—to use one of your American expressions—behind the barn. I was something of what is referred to as a juvenile delinquent. My father disciplined and punished me. He took me out of the public school and placed me in the most regimented Catholic school he could find. My father was a bully," Michel said.

"What about your mother?" Michael asked.

"I spend three weeks out of the year with my mother. I never miss," Michel answered. "Usually during the summer."

"Do you have any brothers or sisters?" I continued.

"One of each."

"Do you spend much time with your brother?"

"No. I am in touch with him maybe once or twice a month."

WE REACHED GREEN ACRES, a small desert town right out of *The Twilight Zone.* Michael interrupted our conversation with polite urgency: *"S'il vous plaît, un moment, j'entends l'appel de la Nature."* Foucault roared with laughter, probably relieved from so much heavy conversation by Michael's playful French.

We alighted from the car into the white heat of midday. The desert air was still and hot as the cinders at the bottom of the pipe, which Mike had extinguished prematurely when he caught sight of the police officer chatting up the service station attendant. We splashed our faces with cold water and drank orange juice filched from the freezer in the trunk.

When we were ready to leave, Michel insisted upon taking the back seat, where, in his new sunglasses, he looked like a creature from outer space. He sat quietly, peering intently through his new sunglasses at the desert horizon while Mike and I carried on an animated conversation about Stockhausen's *Stimmung.*

We decided to picnic overlooking the wide sweep of Panamint Valley, the nearest neighbor to Death Valley, and only a few hours away. At Olancha we turned right onto Route 190 and crossed the desolation of the Owens Lake bed. We reached the lofty Panamint Range and negotiated the narrow dirt road leading to Father Crowley Point, commanding a view of the northern part of Panamint Valley. From there we could see the spot where the Manson family had lived and from whence they had waged war on the earthmovers, which they thought were destroying the landscape.

We spread a blanket in the middle of the small circular bluff, which possessed the intimacy of an eagle's nest, cantilevered over the rockbed five thousand feet below. Foucault darted unceremoniously to the far ledge to gaze into the vast expanse of wind and stone. Just below him the highway spiraled into the capacious valley like an enameled double helix. Foucault stood motionless, transfixed by the colossal rock flow from the northwest into the valley. I gave Foucault a couple of small colorful rocks as a kind of memento of the Panamint. He put them on the dashboard and left them there.

Eventually we sat cross-legged under the summer sun. Mike was afraid Michel's bald head would cause him to suffer heat exhaustion. Michel assured him that he was OK. Mike asked him why his head was bald and he responded with laughter that he had lost so much hair that he'd thought, "Oh, what the heck, I might as well shave it all off." We ate antipasto, hearts of palm, and sourdough bread. Foucault's eyes twinkled approval of the California wine and surveyed the valley like an Indian scout. As usual he dined sparingly.

As we made our way back to the car over the difficult terrain, Foucault asked me if I knew the work of Mark Tobey. I responded that I liked it very much. "For years, I longed to have a painting by him," Foucault said. "At last with the royalties from *The Order of Things* I was able to purchase one of his pictures. An all-white one. It now hangs in my apartment in Paris."

"Have you made much money from your books?" I asked forthrightly.

"Not really. I have not made a lot of money in my life."

The shimmering whiteness of the valley brought to my mind the opening scenes of Antonioni's *The Passenger*. Foucault told me he had not seen it.

I went on to say that Antonioni's *Zabriskie Point*, which I had seen in London in 1970, had made me want to visit California for the first time. Up to then, from my Harvardian perspective, California had seemed a menace to civilization.

Foucault said that he had seen the film, but only on French television. "The small screen and poor reception conspired to diminish the impact of the film," he added. "I have frankly forgotten it."

"Now you will see the real thing and under bizarre conditions. You will probably want to see the film again."

"I intend to."

I took a photograph of the sun. I mentioned to Foucault that Picasso had said in an interview that as a child in Catalonia he had frequently stared straight into the sun. Foucault did not know that anecdote and expressed appreciation that I had related it to him. He was always so happy when someone told him something he thought was useful or interesting to know.

WE STARTED THE FINAL LAP to the entrance of Death Valley, where we would make our journey into the center of Earth. Slowly we made our way to the top of Towne Pass, five thousand feet above sea level. Pausing for an instant, we gazed at the parabolic expanse of the earth before us. On our left a gigantic mass of slate and limestone bisected two enormous mountain ranges, the Grapevines and the

Cottonwoods, and then cascaded into the Mesquite Flat Sand Dunes. Death Valley bored into the earth like a solar plexus enclosed by the Black Mountains on the far horizon and the jagged ridges of the Panamint Range to our right.

As we sped down the narrow asphalt road I mentioned to Foucault that this was only my third visit to Death Valley, yet I felt I was returning to the elementary basis of my subconscious mind. "Mystical" was the only word I could find to do justice to my experience here. Mike agreed with me.

Reaching the floor of the valley about midafternoon, we cruised through Stovepipe Wells Village. Once beyond the village we passed the outcrop of sand dunes, which shift continuously across the valley floor. We sped through the Devil's Cornfield, a plantation of arrow-weed, which the Indians in the area smoked as a tranquilizer. We continued along Route 190, making a sharp right turn taking us southwest through the center of the valley along the precise line of sea level.

After a few miles we caught sight of boulders forming colonnades around a small lake. The cyprinodont, an ancient fish, resides there—living fossils a million years old. They are believed to be descended from the fishes of a vast lake that lay between these mountains at the end of the last ice age.

Some miles ahead we glimpsed a grove of palm trees, glimmering like a mirage. They surround the Furnace Creek ranch, a resort located within an oasis. It was 115 degrees Fahrenheit as we drove through the abundant oleander bushes in full bloom. After checking into our room, we decided to luxuriate for an hour or so in the air conditioning. Michel took a nap while Michael and I perused Daumier's *Lib Women*, a book Foucault had brought to us from San Francisco.

THE ARTIST'S PALETTE

Refreshed, we headed for the Artist's Palette, an alluvial fan at the base of a canyon about five miles south of the Furnace Creek ranch. Turning left on Artist's Drive, we negotiated through a narrow corridor between enormous boulders until we reached the observation point overlooking a rainbow of Precambrian ores oxidized by the millennia into iridescent hillocks scattered over the lap of the canyon. Some of the hills are small enough for playing King of the Mountain, while others can be scaled to heights commanding the valley. The whole area was deserted.

We took the path bordered by silver atriplex. Leopard lizards skittered helter-skelter. Michael took out the magical potion while Foucault looked on intently. I could hear in my mind's ear the strains of the Liebesnacht from *Tristan und Isolde*.

Foucault appeared troubled, and with grim countenance he walked away. Michael and I conferred about his state of mind. We both knew that the potion taken under any kind of duress can discompose the unwilling. We certainly would not wish to force anything upon Michel. Foucault returned shortly and with quizzical eyes declared that he wished to take only half as much, since this was his first experience with a potion so powerful.

I took Michel by the arm and we walked together for a spell. I sympathized with his anxiety but assured him that the impact of the trip would be appreciably diminished if he took anything less than the prescribed amount. For a few long moments he pondered my words, then abruptly walked back to Michael and inquired about the proper way of ingesting it.

Following instructions, he wet the tip of his finger, then pressed down the substance against his bottom teeth and gulped audibly. Then close together we three walked deeper into the Artist's Palette, which glittered in the beam of the setting sun like a mosaic tomb illuminated by an excavator's torch.

As we climbed down the embankment to the canyon floor, Foucault was silent and withdrawn. Michael carried his little black bag with the accoutrements that would guarantee a smooth journey. Safely at the bottom of the canyon we began to thread our way along a slender path flanked by massive rocks protruding over us like eaves.

"How long before the potion begins to take effect?" Michel inquired.

"From twenty to thirty minutes," Michael responded. "But we will help it along with grass and liqueur."

We reached a cleft between a procession of orange and purple hills. We sat in the soft gravel. Michael lit a pipe. He assured Foucault that a few tokes would facilitate his journey into higher consciousness.

Next, Michael opened his satchel and produced three plastic cups and a bottle of Grand Marnier. I flipped out a coveted gold-tipped jasmine cigarette, which Michael and I shared alone since Michel did not smoke tobacco. Soon we were submerged in a confluence of glorious fragrances.

Michel settled comfortably into a crevice between two mounds of turquoise blue. Though his eyes were alert, he was silent and appeared slightly perplexed. My anxiety about his diffidence was somewhat assuaged when he reached energetically for the pipe, took a long toke, and then passed it grinning like the Cheshire cat.

"It is very difficult to find pure drugs in France," Michel said, evidently considering the heavenly elixir to have druglike properties. He sipped his Grand Marnier slowly. "Even the good stuff available in France ends up in America. I do not understand it. Not that I have not had the opportunity to try all manner of things in France. I have been to parties where I was even offered LSD, but as I told you, I was with my lover, who refused for both of us. Perhaps he resists hallucinogens because he has a certain way of relating to his body. After all, we are our bodies!" Foucault paused and then added, "And something else."

That's it, I thought. That is the revolution in consciousness that Foucault has proclaimed. All other philosophers in the West have started and ended in the mind, in ideas. Foucault affirms the primacy of the body and power of discourse.

"I am presently writing a book about the body," Foucault said.

"I am anxious to read it. With this definition of human nature," I said, "you have shattered the entire Western philosophical tradition. Since my first Death Valley trip, I have been asking myself why from Plato onward philosophers and theologians have so consistently reviled the body and lionized the geist."

Foucault seemed to agree with my assessment but did not pursue the subject any further. He obviously did not want to talk about philosophy. Michel and Mike went off on their own. I watched them poke in and out of the rock chambers, stop to examine a constellation of striated pebbles lying on the ground, then climb another miniature mountain to glimpse a distant peak towering on the ink-blue horizon. The brightly colored strata of the canyon walls fluttered like streamers in a parade.

I asked Foucault to join me on a ledge affording a vista of the desert floor hundreds of feet below us. He climbed the steep grade with the agility of an acrobat. On the horizon directly in front of us the sun scraped the top of Telescope Peak and bled into the valley twelve thousand feet below. Michael sat on the pinnacle of a nearby hill and switched on his portable tape recorder. As we watched the shadows lengthen over the alkaline flats, the dissonances of Charles Ives's *Three Places in New England* reverberated through the canyon walls. Foucault and I began to laugh ecstatically as the sound swept through us into the salt flats glistening like icing on a wedding cake.

"You know," Foucault said, "Genet prefers laughter to sex."

The irony that the great writer about sex actually preferred to laugh made everything seem even funnier. We gazed in front of us upon a mountain that took on the contours of a Mayan pyramid.

"Has any other age, any other time, perceived the earth as we do now?" I asked Foucault.

"No," he answered firmly. "At no time in history has anyone seen the earth as this concoction, as this moment together allows us to see it now."

After rambling over and through the hills for a while Michael indicated that it was time to leave.

"Leave!" Foucault said in amazement. "How can we leave such beauty? Why don't we just stay here. I cannot imagine finding a more lovely place."

Eventually Mike convinced him. We made our way down the circuitous alley, winding around imposing monoliths contoured like Henry Moore sculptures. I looked back to see how Michel was faring. Lingering, he was grazing his hands along the grizzled textures of the rocks. I uttered some words of Heraclitus: "The fairest universe is but a heap of rubbish." He smiled. Once we reached the parking lot, we could not resist turning around for one long last look at the glorious palette assuming its crepuscular hue.

ZABRISKIE POINT

As we motored slowly along Artist's Drive, I felt I was on a carnival ride through the grotto of Leonardo's *Madonna of the Rocks.* Each object was clear and distinct. Everything seemed artificial. I was experiencing the phenomena on many levels simultaneously, as if my mind were an eight-track tape, each sensation with multiple channels of its own. I could speak, think, desire, hear, see, feel, imagine, remember on many discrete levels that connected to marvelous effect. Unimaginable synesthesia, immense worlds of delight, Proustian paradise found.

With some relief at having steered safely through the desert reef, we stopped momentarily upon reaching the highway and inhaled the cool air blowing across the alkaline pools. We made a sharp right turn and drove north on Route 178. Michael slowed down so we could get a good look at Mushroom Rock.

We passed Golden Canyon displaying its sequined tapestries. To our left we surveyed the Devil's Golf Course, an expanse of salt crystals, which resembles a frozen metropolis viewed from a satellite. From our vantage point we could see the desert floor dramatically descend to the lowest point of elevation in North America, about three hundred feet below sea level. The distant mountains showed forth a rainbow of myriad colors undulating in harmony with fluorescent clouds racing through the sky.

"The decorative rhythms of clouds and strata bring Gauguin to mind," I said. "How could Artaud have held such disdain for Gauguin, whom he dubbed a painter of ghosts when he compared him to Van Gogh?"

"Oh, that Artaud was such a snob," Foucault replied. "Van Gogh was just coming into fashion when he wrote that piece, and Artaud wanted to be ahead of everyone else."

"Everything is either art nouveau or art deco," Michael intoned philosophically.

"You are saying either organic or geometric," I commented. Then suddenly my attention was arrested by fantastic faces formed by shadows burrowing into the mountain façades. I mentioned the opening scene of *Zardoz* with its Magrittian depiction of a monumental stone sphinx sailing in the air.

Foucault, who did not know the film, said, "*The Castle of the Pyrenees* is one of my favourite paintings by Magritte. I have seen the original hanging in New York, in a lawyer's apartment. He also had some other masterpieces by Magritte. It was marvelous seeing all those paintings in one place."

"I have just read your little book on Magritte," I said. "I was surprised that you find Kandinsky and Klee the two generative forces in modern art. I would have thought Picasso and Duchamp. But your book gave me a fresh perspective on Magritte."

"I am totally intrigued by Magritte. I have received several interesting letters from him," Foucault continued. "Their contents were so subtle and obscure that I am not sure whether I understood them. At one point Magritte said that artists can be divided into groups: those who reach for 'similitude' and those who portray 'resemblance.' He thinks the thrust of Western art is toward the former. But Magritte claimed that he portrayed resemblance, the better to convey real experience rather than mere likeness."

We reached Route 190 and, turning right, sped by the Furnace Creek Inn. After a short drive we arrived at Zabriskie Point. I shivered with apprehension about ascending the steep grade leading to the small circular parking lot overlooking the sandstone sea. We inched our way to the circular barrier of the overview, which resembled the hub of a flying saucer. We alighted from the car as if explorers on a forbidden planet.

WE WERE ALONE. The area appeared barren of life. The sky over the crests of the Panamint Mountains glowed blue white in the darkening sky, and the salt pools twinkled in the distance beyond the thrust of Manley Beacon, an enormous rock formation that marks the place like the Parthenon defines the Acropolis.

We huddled together beside the low wall separating us from the abyss of interlocking canyons below. Michael brought out the tape deck and asked us to choose between Stockhausen's *Hymnen* and Richard Strauss's *Four Last Songs*. Without hesitation Foucault chose the latter.

Michel and Michael sat side by side on the granite parapet. The dunes seemed to rise and fall in counterpoint to the voice of Elizabeth Schwarzkopf. Venus appeared above Telescope Peak and sparkled ever so brightly. Soon she was encircled by a garland of stars. With the final words of the last song—"Come nearer, gentle peace / profound in the glow of evening. / How weary we are of wandering. / Is this perhaps death?"—we reached a transcendent congruence of place, mood, and music.

"Music is our theology," Foucault said quietly.

"Michel," Mike asked, "would you care for a cold soft drink?"

"No," he responded emphatically. "I do not want anything to come between me and the drug and what's out there. I do not want anything to interfere with the pure experience of the drug."

Then Foucault turned to me and said with a quizzical tone, "Simeon, why are you drinking that stuff?"

"Oh, it's just another kind of chemical," I said. Feeling that I had said something stupid, I drew close to Michel for some reassurance. Michel, who was propped on his elbow against the parapet, reminded me of *The Sleeping Gypsy*. He seemed to welcome our intimacy.

"Michel," I asked, "in your life was there a specific event—say, something like Rousseau on the road to Vincennes, or St. Paul on his way to Damascus, even Buddha under the Bodhi tree—that afforded you the crucial insight that would determine the direction of your work?"

"Yes!" he responded. "When I enrolled at the École normale the headmaster demanded to learn if there was anything unusual about me. When I informed him of my homosexuality, he replied with horrified expression that such behavior was not normal and certainly unacceptable to the reputation of the school. He then had me confined, for my own good, he said. He told me that I must be reformed, that I would be confined, examined, and treated by an array of authorities—doctors, teachers, psychologist, psychiatrists, etc. At this instant I recognized in a flash how the system works. I perceived the fundamental impulse of our society: *normalization.*"

"Had you fallen in love with another man by then?"

"I first fell in love with a man when I was sixteen. Since that time I have always moved from *love* to *knowledge* to *truth.*"

When Michael walked to the car to get some more tapes, Foucault remarked, "Michael is wonderful. He is a wizard. He is always conjuring up something for us."

WE FELL SILENT to listen to Stockhausen's *Song of the Youths.* Zabriskie Point was filled with the sounds of a kindergarten playground overlaid with electronic tonalities. *Kontakte* followed. Glissandos bounced off the stars, which glowed like incandescent pinballs. Foucault turned to Michael and said that this was the first time he really understood what Stockhausen had achieved.

I lay on my back, looked into the heavens, and felt I was hallucinating. Booming, buzzing, and flashing, the whole sky became a penny arcade. I thought Warhol, Warhol. The stars assumed the shape of enormous Christmas tree ornaments moving in formation slowly and gracefully through the moonless sky. Complete tranquility enveloped me. I knew that the heavenly elixir allowed me to see the total spectra of each star. The lustrous colors radiated outward to form the illusion of solid, luminescent spheres.

I turned to Michel and said in trembling voice, "We have conceived the universe—a majestic procession of beautiful trifles, a timeless spectacle. This vision makes everything else seem like a big joke."

Foucault smiled and made a sweeping gaze of the heavens. "The sky has exploded and the stars are raining down upon me. I know this is not true, but it is the Truth."

"Do you think it would be possible for the whole of humanity to take this concoction and to experience something on the order of what we are doing here tonight?" I asked.

"I would like it to be possible," Foucault responded wistfully.

"Are you sure you do not think that others in past time have had similar experiences to ours tonight? After all, John Allegro has shown that from the Sumerians to the Essenes to modern times, there is a direct line of communities who have used the amanita muscaria, which is another kind of elixir."

Again, Foucault assured me that we are different and that no one before could have had this kind of experience.

"Duchamp," I said, "thought that after the original excitement of discovery, psychedelic mushrooms and similar kinds of plants would be used sparingly like liqueurs."

"At last I understand the meaning of Lowry's *Under the Volcano,*" Foucault declared. "The Consul's mescal served as a drug that filtered his perception in a manner similar to a hallucinogen. The only thing I can compare this experience to in my life is sex with a stranger. Contact with a strange body affords an experience of the Truth similar to what I am experiencing now."

Michel rose to his feet and walked a few yards away to lie down alongside the barrier. "Michael," he said from a distance, "why didn't you bring any of your music to play for us?"

"I did bring one short tape," Michael responded. He went to the car and returned with his "Praeludium on a Theme by Bach." The wind picked up and the car began to rock.

"Why do you keep opening the car doors, Simeon?" Michael asked in an imploring voice. "I close them, then you go open them. You are going to run down the battery."

"To have the car light on," I said. "It is so dark and the wind is so strong. Don't you think we are in danger from the wind up here, Michel?" I asked, angling for support.

"Don't be scared," Foucault said. "The wind feels mild and warm to me."

After a long period of silence we drew close to Michel. "I am very happy," he told us, tears streaming from his eyes. "Tonight I have achieved a fresh perspective on myself. I now understand my sexuality. It all seems to start with my sister. We *must* go home again." Then he repeated the last statement, "Yes, we must go home again."

"I was wrong," I said, "to use the word 'mystical' to describe this experience."

Foucault agreed.

"Do you think this event will affect your work?" I asked.

"Definitely," he replied.

"Have you had any philosophical insights tonight?" I inquired.

"Not really. I have not spent these hours reflecting on concepts. It has not been a philosophical experience for me, but something else entirely."

Michael suggested that we should return to the motel and get some rest.

"If you like," Michel said. "I could stay here the rest of the night, but I am ready to go whenever you and Simeon wish."

DANTE'S VIEW

When we returned to the Furnace Creek ranch, Foucault took a shower and had a brief nap in his bright-red jockey shorts. I went outside and stupidly wasted time preparing an introductory speech for Foucault's lecture in Claremont that evening. Mike studied Japanese.

At breakfast a few hours later, I asked Foucault how he could explain the startling eruption of genius in history. "A Pascal, a Hölderlin, for example; where do they come from?"

Foucault said, "History does not move like this," and using his index finger he made a movement in a straight line. "It moves like this." His finger randomly stabbed the air. He was indicating total dispersion. Witnessing his frenzied gesture I felt certain that the Age of History was over because its most basic assumption, the Spencerian notion of the steady, progressive development of humanity, had been shattered by Michel Foucault.

We returned to Zabriskie Point for a daytime view. We were still in a kind of visionary trance, but of course the peak period was over. I took pictures and Foucault was very cooperative. He smiled a lot. Then we were off. We drove along Route 190, passed Twenty Mule Team Canyon, and reached the turnoff for Dante's View, our destination about twenty miles away. I speculated that some early prospectors had given the observation point the name Dante's View because of the similarity between the vista and Gustave Doré's etchings depicting Dante's *Inferno*.

Except for the creosote and buckwheat bushes clinging to the slopes, which descend precipitously toward the salt flats more than five thousand feet below, we were surrounded by a kingdom of naked rocks and peaks. Looking west toward the Pacific Ocean you see seven or more mountain ranges, including the razor-sharp spires of the Sierra Nevada. Gazing east in the direction of Arizona you see a vast luminescent desert punctuated by dry hills and dormant volcanoes. The view is like Altdorfer's famous painting minus any signs of life.

Michel and I took a narrow path leading to a perch cantilevered over the valley. It could have been an eagle's nest, so snug and precarious were its boundaries. Foucault was intrepid and insisted on leading me to the very edge, where one wrong move could have sent us both hurtling straight into the inferno below.

Here at last I was able to practice the discipline of keeping silent. We sat side by side for an hour listening to the wind pierced by the cry of birds sailing through the void. Foucault would peer intently into the abyss below. Then his gaze would rise to meet the mountains, which seemed to speak to him. For a while he would focus on the broad swath of salt flats glimmering in the distance like a frozen inland sea. Sometimes he seemed to be looking at nothing.

Foucault hardly moved. His face was impassive. When we rose to leave, all I could muster to describe the majestic desolation was "O brave new world." Michel looked directly into my eyes and then in deep meditation he walked back alone. I should have finished the line from the *Tempest*: "...that has such people in it."

When we reached the car, Michael was cheerfully taking a sunbath while reading T. S. Eliot's *Four Quartets* and listening to Boulez's *Pli selon pli*. Still tripping, I saw through the eyes of Maxfield Parrish, Michael's glabrous body languishing against the translucent blue sky.

"This is one of my favorite pieces of music," Michel said to Mike as we approached the car. "Do you know Boulez's *Le Marteau sans maître*?"

"I have heard it a couple of times, but I am only beginning to appreciate Boulez," Michael responded.

"Really, I do wish you would study with Boulez in Paris," Michel rejoined.

"I know I would like that very much," Michael replied. "Do you know the *Four Quartets*?"

"Not really," Michel answered.

"Perhaps when we get home we will have time to listen to a recording of Eliot reading his poems. I have written a poem about our last trip to Death Valley. From the vantage point of Dante's View you might like the last line: 'The dry lake is but the flood forgotten.'"

After a quick lunch spread out over the trunk of the car we set off for home. We retraced our route past Zabriskie Point, the Furnace Creek ranch, and the Mesquite Flat Sand Dunes. We agreed to take a different route back. Before taking the driver's seat I grabbed a few cookies. "Our boy likes cookies," Foucault remarked with an indulgent smile.

Then he added, "I can see that you two have enjoyed yourselves very much. Where did you say you met?"

"The 4709 Club," Mike answered.

"That place will be very famous," Foucault assured us.

"You mean notorious, *n'est-ce pas*?" I said with a laugh.

"No, I mean famous," Foucault said seriously.

I thought, If only because we have tripped with Michel Foucault.

"We will give you some stuff to take with you to Paris," Mike said.

"Thank you. I would like that. Do you think I should tell others about our trip, the special nature of our trip, when we get back?" Foucault inquired pensively.

"I would hope so," I responded.

A PARTY

We returned in time for Foucault to give his scheduled talk in a hall holding hundreds of eager faces. He was irritable and insisted upon speaking in French. Mike refused to attend. I was mortified because I knew Foucault hated large crowds and that the Claremont crowd hated me because it was obvious that Michel and I had been up to no good. Foucault made the best of it and spoke eloquently if haltingly about the nature of power in contemporary society. The interpreter had a difficult time of it. The crowd grew restive, so I abruptly adjourned the session.

As we were leaving the hall, Foucault expressed disappointment about his performance. He complained that throughout the discussion he was besieged by waves of sleep and that there were times when he did not feel he could proceed any further. I explained to him that he was crashing but that his energy would return when the surroundings became pleasant again.

We returned to the house, where a party in his honor was in progress. Mike had festooned the ceilings with eucalyptus branches. I had invited a rock band from Hollywood for the pleasure of the guests, which numbered a hundred or more. Foucault mixed easily among the crowd. The youthful spirit of California blossomed for Foucault that night. Foucault responded with frequent smiles and animated conversation. Questions about his impressions of California proliferated.

"I love California," he reiterated many times. "You live in one of the choice places on Earth." He continually stressed how much he liked the variety and experimentation in lifestyles, as well as the marvelous climate, which allows people to stay in touch with the body, to literally *see* the body.

"And you have such intellectual freedom and vitality here," he said. "Ideological dogma and partisanship are still so rampant in France that compared to California we live in France under an intellectual reign of terror."

"Are there parties like this in France?" a student asked Michel.

"No, the French are still too stuffy," Michel answered tersely with a smile.

Another student confessed that he had not read any of Michel's books.

"But you do not need to read my books," Michel reassured him.

A young woman asked him for an opinion on women's liberation.

"I will say this," he responded. "Women must not ignore the fact that they have had great power in our society. They have reared the children."

"In your talk this evening you spoke of the 'great genius of Sartre,'" a professor broke into the group to say. "What do you think of the *Critique de la raison dialectique*?"

"On several occasions I have tried to read it, but I can never get any farther than the first fifty pages. I doubt if I will make another attempt."

Another self-important tenured professor swaggered over and blubbered, "What is your opinion of Camus?"

"It would have been interesting to see what Camus would have done during the Algerian revolution. What a disappointment when he received the Nobel Prize for Literature as a Frenchman when it was awarded to him as both a Frenchman and an Algerian. That might indicate where his allegiances would have been during the civil war."

In a conversation with Brit, the student who first pointed out Foucault to me at Irvine, Michel asked him what he was studying. Brit told him that he was in the European Studies Program. Brit then asked what he thought about concentrating in literature as a graduate student.

"You should not waste your time studying literature as a discipline," he said. "Study the power mechanisms at work in our speech and our society."

"What has been your impression of Stanford?" Phyllis Johnson, whose girlfriend was thinking about teaching there, inquired. Foucault made a square with his hands. The laughter drowned out the music.

"Yes, square," Foucault said. "But I am very interested in what is happening at Berkeley," he added. "It is a place to watch, a sort of microcosm of the contemporary university. When I gave a public lecture at Berkeley shortly after arriving I felt a great distance from the audience. The whole affair was very stiff and formal. At Irvine it was better. The group seemed more responsive. Stanford, on the other hand, struck me as hopeless, even sterile."

"Yes, much like here," I interjected. "How do you like teaching at Berkeley?"

"Well, the French department at Berkeley hired me to teach literature, but that was all wrong, since I don't like literature. They are a little annoyed with me up there because most of the students in my course are from the history department."

"What happened at the university in Berkeley when Saigon fell to the North Vietnamese and the Americans pulled out of Vietnam?" I asked.

"Nothing happened at all. No-*thing*!" he said to emphasize his disappointment. "Apparently the notion is still current among Europeans that Berkeley is as radical as it was in the sixties."

Al Franken, the comedian who would later shine on *Saturday Night Live* and then go on to become a US Senator, asked Michel which team he thought would win the World Series. Michel laughed and, humorously echoing his remark at the previous lecture, disclaimed being a prophet. But he assured Al that he was interested in sports and kept in shape by cycling and doing gymnastics.

Immediately a group of students asked him if he would like to go cycling the next day on the strenuous Glendora Ridge Road nearby. Michel expressed enthusiasm about the proposal but doubted he would have time, since he had to return to San Francisco the following afternoon.

AT ONE POINT during the evening Foucault went to the front porch, stretched out full length on the balustrade, and gazed at the moon.

"I am trying to recapture my state of mind in Death Valley," he told me. "But it is very difficult. I can't seem to do it without the aid of the hallucinogen."

A few times Michel conveyed an unspoken appreciation when I would rescue him from a barrage of philosophical questions. But he was consistently courteous, even with the overzealous interlocutors. After spending some time with a small group of men and women, one of the men leaned over and kissed Michel on the lips. Michel returned the kiss with unaffected tenderness. Then the small group brought Foucault into their circle for several rounds of kisses and embraces.

A young man approached Foucault and told him that he had just come out—that is to say, he had professed his homosexuality. He thanked Foucault for his work, for he believed that he "made things like gay liberation possible."

Foucault responded by saying, "This is a nice thing to say to me, but really my work has had nothing to do with gay liberation. I have written nothing on the subject."

"What was it like for you before the gay movement?" the young gay student asked.

"You might not believe this," Foucault replied, "but I actually liked the scene before gay liberation, when everything was more covert. It was like an underground fraternity, exciting and a bit dangerous. Friendship meant a lot, it meant a lot of trust, we protected each other, we related to each other by secret codes."

"What do you think about gay liberation now?"

"First of all, I believe that the term 'gay' has become obsolete—and indeed all such terms denoting a specific sexual orientation. The reason for this is the transformation of our understanding of sexuality. We see the extent to which our pursuit of pleasure has been limited in large part by a vocabulary foisted upon us. People are neither this nor that, gay or straight. There is an infinite range of what we call sexual behavior, and terms that prevent this range from being put into play—that is to say, terms that stereotype behavior, that are wrong and misleading."

"Secondly," Michel went on to say, "what I like about California is that the word 'homosexual' doesn't mean very much here anymore. People in California don't seem to have that word in their vocabulary. It seems to me that when people use the word 'homosexual' or 'gay,' it is in the context of speaking of someone who should be excluded. This has been transcended in California. There is a freedom in talking about homosexuality here. The word is not pejorative. The idea is not associated with perversion."

"Still," the student pressed on, "do you read the literature of gay liberation? The *Advocate*, for example?"

"By all means. I subscribe to the *Advocate* and read it closely," he replied.

At one o'clock in the morning I asked Michel if he would like to get back to the motel for some rest. He told me that he would be happy to walk back, but of course I insisted upon driving him. A few minutes later he said he was ready to go. The house was still jammed with revelers.

I hoped to encourage a general exodus by announcing in stentorian voice that Michel was leaving. He was visibly taken aback by my brazenness in calling attention to his departure, and I felt no little embarrassment at my own audacity. At that moment I realized just how much Michel hated the spotlight. Clearly he was bewildered that I should inform the group that he was leaving.

But one good consequence of my gaffe ensued. Just as we were walking out the door my friend David, a mountain man, approached Michel. He told Michel that he regretted he had not taken the opportunity to engage him in conversation that evening, but he wanted him to know how much his books meant to him and how much he appreciated his visit to Claremont. Michel thanked him and as soon as we were in the car asked me, with a quality of enthusiasm I had not encountered in him thus far, to provide some information about the young man he had just spoken with.

"He is a graduate student in the European Studies Program," I told Foucault. "His master's thesis is a comparison between your work and R. D. Laing's. We have known each other for three years now. We met back East, and it was our friendship that brought me to California. This summer he is living in a mountain cabin not too far from here."

Foucault's eyes twinkled. When I suggested that in the morning we take a hike to David's cabin in Bear Canyon, Foucault volunteered a spirited assent.

BEAR CANYON TRAILS

The next morning, Michel said he had not been able to sleep. Almost at once upon returning to his bleak motel room he had wished himself back at the party. He had almost walked back, so unhappy he was at missing out on the good time he could still have had there. Yet, even without much rest he was chipper and relaxed.

We set off for the mountains and in fifteen minutes were ascending Mount Baldy Road, over which yellow spears of flowering Scottish broom arched liked a canopy. We reached Baldy Village and turned left by the fire station onto the narrow road leading to the parking lot at the entrance of Bear Canyon. There we joined up with a group of six young men, four of whom lived in cabins throughout the canyon, composing a kind of Taoist commune. The sound of waterfalls beckoned us to the trail flanked by large cedars and Ponderosa pines. The musky smell of the chaparral was a pungent aphrodisiac.

We ambled through the forest, and as the ascent became steeper we moved in single file along the rocky trail from which we could see the sparkling stream. The high desert wildflowers were in blossom.

Fiery Indian paintbrush and pale-yellow phlox graced our path. Foucault spoke amiably with his companions. In about an hour we reached the uppermost cabin, where we surprised its Taoist denizen.

"David," I called, as Skadi, my dog, ran to meet his dog, Krina. "I have brought you Michel." And there in the glade where David and I had spoken so often about Michel Foucault, we now had the great man in person. It was something of an incarnation, "the word made flesh."

David, tall, broad-shouldered, slim-waisted, resplendently naked except for a pair of brief cut-off jeans, opened the door and stepped out on the porch, which jutted out over the streambed. "Welcome!" he called back excitedly. "I'll put on some coffee."

We piled into the cabin as David put away the yoga pad he had been using for his morning exercise. He showed Michel the kitchen replete with stove and fridge. He took him up the ladder to the loft and pointed out the large skylights he had put in himself. Then we followed him to the first floor of the cabin, where there is a shower with the luxury of hot water. Next, we sat before the fire in the living room and listened to the stereo, first some country music, then some Mozart and Mahler. Finally, David beckoned us to the porch for a view of the stream tumbling beneath us. The porch was a virtual treehouse perched amidst the tops of gigantic pines and cedars. Eventually everybody assembled there for coffee and conversation.

Cal, a stocky, well-built man in his early thirties, sat next to Michel. He sported a spiffy mustache, studied psychology, and lived with a group of friends in a house surrounded by orange trees. Recently Cal had taken LSD and received such a troubling vision of his family that he began to do some investigating. He found out that his father, whom he had placed on a pedestal, was in fact a mean, mercenary man hated by his employees and despised by his peers. This discovery led to a breakdown. Recently he had come to our house late at night, sat on the porch, and wept bitterly about his disillusionment. After comforting him with some Laingian analysis about the politics of experience, I took him back to his new family in the orange grove.

Next to Cal, a much younger man, Chris by name, smoked a cigarette while staring into the entrails of the stream. Chris lived in the cabin about thirty yards away through the dense foliage. He had bought the cabin when he graduated from high school, and for the last two years he had worked incessantly to make it distinctive and commodious. A blond surfer type in a strong, wiry body, he had a sweet anorexic girlfriend who liked to sunbathe naked on the rocks in the middle of the stream in front of their cabin. Chris played the guitar and read voraciously. In his mountain retreat he studied the human sciences. Frequently he joined David and me for our discussions at night by the fire.

Chris was speaking with his friend John, who also lived in the canyon nearby. John had the temerity to gather some of his friends and pull his piano a mile up the steep trail to his cabin. Sometimes late at night the importunate sounds of jazz piano alternating with Chopin nocturnes wafted through the vale. John was a short man who wore dirty pants and sported an enormous phallus, which he enjoyed in a sleazy kind of way. He had serious musical aspirations and loved to listen to our discussions about literature and philosophy. Living through the freezing winters in the mountains had given him a sinus problem, so he tended to wheeze and snort from time to time, but his gross habits were a kind of charm that would be missed.

Jake adorned the scene with his unbared hairy chest capped by a puckish smile. He was a biker and an atypical undergraduate at the Claremont Men's College. Mike and I were teaching him hatha yoga and he was teaching us physics. We had just taught him the cat position, which suited him perfectly. He was fascinated with the idea of entropy, which he couldn't quite figure out. Recently Jake gave me a bear hug and with tears in his eyes did something very few students are wont to do. He thanked me, especially for trying to live what I teach, unlike his other teachers, whom he considered automatons spouting empty words. In return I asked him if I could graze my hands in his thick, hairy chest. He consented bashfully. I thought Foucault might like this man.

Lance was an exceedingly attractive man, medium height, bubble butt, a skier and all-around athlete. He was a student at Pomona College and attended Michael's music class at the house. He seemed such an anomaly because he combined serious intellectual and musical interests with the panache of a preppy and a paucity of learning, two traits that seem to be encouraged by his college. Lance was just coming to terms with his homosexuality. "After all," he had said to me, "I spend most of my time with men, why shouldn't I make love with them?" With his inquiring blue eyes and extraordinary good looks, Lance was a welcome member of Foucault's entourage.

Finally, there was Jim, who was a ceramicist and graduate student in philosophy. A carpenter by profession, he exuded a quality of

Reichian energy that was irresistible. After he came to class with a pair of Levi's with a hole in the crotch, I had always sought to lecture from a vantage point close to his chair. On some days I felt I was just speaking about schizoanalysis and political anatomy to him alone. There were days when the prospect of coming in touch with his being was the only reason I could muster to show up for class. He lived with his girlfriend in a treehouse at the entrance to the canyon. Sharon had been a hippie political activist in the sixties, but LSD and Jim had changed her into a mountain recluse.

FOUCAULT GRACIOUSLY ENGAGED the Taoist band with what the French call "*saveur*," an abundant graciousness. He was to use another French term, "*disponible*," open to everything. He expressed amazement to find such comfortable accommodations in the mountain wilderness. "It has the feeling of *Swiss Family Robinson*," Foucault remarked.

"Do you like that story?" David asked.

"Yes, even as a child. Of course, I was told that I should prefer *Robinson Crusoe*, but actually I liked *Swiss Family Robinson* a lot more, and still do."

I told Michel that during the years we lived together up here David and I often felt like castaways. We passed the time giving each other back rubs and discussing books and the world in front of the fire every evening.

"Just a few nights ago the roaring fire prompted a conversation about Gaston Bachelard's *Psychoanalysis of Fire*," I said to Foucault. "Did you by chance know Bachelard?"

"Yes, I did," Foucault responded. "He was my teacher and exerted a great influence upon me."

"I can just visualize Bachelard musing before his hearth and devising the startling thesis that mankind tamed fire to stimulate his daydreaming, that man is fundamentally the dreaming animal."

"Not really," Foucault blurted out. "Bachelard probably never saw a fireplace or ever listened to water streaming down a mountainside. With him it was all a dream. He lived very ascetically in a cramped two-room flat he shared with his sister."

"I have read somewhere that he was a gourmet and would shop every day in the street markets to get the freshest produce for his dinner."

"Well, he undoubtedly shopped in the outdoor markets," Foucault responded impatiently, "but his cuisine, like his regimen, was very plain. He led a simple life and existed in his dream."

"Do you shop in the outdoor markets in Paris?" Jake asked Michel.

"No," Foucault laughed, "I just go to the supermarket down the street from where I live."

Foucault noticed a copy of *National Geographic* nearby. "Wouldn't you say that is a good magazine?" he asked. We all agreed. Spotting a copy of a newspaper headline about Israel and Lebanon prompted him to exclaim that he followed the events in Israel very closely.

"I am very sympathetic to Israel. I saw such unbelievable suffering among the Jews during World War II," he said. "The Jews must survive."

"Do you read a newspaper regularly?" Jake asked.

"Yes, I read *Le Monde* every day," Foucault replied.

Jake told Foucault that even though he followed political events very closely and had been involved in the anti–Vietnam War movement, he felt that he was completely lost.

"'You have to be lost as a young man," Michel replied. "'You are not really trying unless you are lost. That is a good sign. I was lost as a young man too.'"

"Should I take chances with my life?" Jake continued.

"By all means! Take risks, go out on a limb."

"But I yearn for solutions."

"There are no solutions."

"Then at least some answers."

"There are no answers!"

After his exchange with Jake, Foucault joined David before the fire in the living room of the cabin. While they got acquainted, the rest of the group scattered into the surrounding woods looking for mushrooms and firewood.

ON THE PORCH

Eventually the Bear Canyon band gathered again on the porch to speak with Foucault. Jim, the philosopher carpenter, waxed enthusiastic about the French thinker Merleau-Ponty. Foucault acknowledged with evident enthusiasm that Merleau-Ponty was one of his most important teachers.

"In fact," Michel went on to say, "Merleau-Ponty was much more influential for my generation than Sartre. He was a rigorous scholar that we all could admire. He combined extensive knowledge with practical politics. He helped to release the stranglehold of Stalinist Marxism and encouraged us to seek a fresh understanding of Marx."

"Do you accept Merleau-Ponty's idea of cultural sediment?" Jim inquired.

"I would put it in these terms," Foucault answered. "We do not have a private discourse, but we are born into a discourse."

"Therefore, we must listen to others to understand ourselves," Jim said.

"Yes, precisely," Foucault said.

"How would you compare him to Sartre?" Chris asked.

"Well, Sartre is the last of the prophets and much more abstruse than Merleau-Ponty."

"Have you read Sartre's *Critique de la raison dialectique*?" Chris inquired.

"I told someone at Michael and Simeon's party that I had once read the first chapter twice and was never able to get any farther. The problem with Sartre is that he never acquainted himself with the knowledge produced by twentieth-century historians. He was convinced by Marx and never got any further. Consequently, his understanding of history was negligible. We cannot learn anything from Sartre's historical analysis."

"Would you agree that Fernand Braudel is the greatest twentieth-century historian?" Jim asked.

Foucault replied, "I guess so."

"Don't you think that existentialism has degenerated into a kind of hedonism, an obsession with one's own lived experience at the expense of work, study, and observation?" Jake, the hairy biker, wondered aloud.

"Yes," Foucault responded. "We have forgotten how to work hard, and existentialism must be combatted on those grounds as well as others."

"And what of Gramsci?" Cal added.

"Gramsci was much more important to me when I was younger and in the Communist Party," Foucault replied. "Gramsci legitimized dissent in the Communist Party at a time when one was compelled to footnote every position taken. At least we could footnote Gramsci as a dissenter within the Marxist paradigm. And his work is itself intrinsically important, particularly as a precedent. In the fifties the Marxists were totally involved with the debate on Stalin. Gramsci helped us out of that imbroglio. He gave dissent, let us say, a foot in the door."

Cal asked Foucault if he thought Marx really distinguished infrastructure from superstructure.

Foucault replied, "In the first place Marx did not write books for our edification or for scholarly exegesis but to get something done, to start something, to speak to workers. So we ought not to treat Marx as a text. Do we need an interpreter like Althusser to tell us what Marx *really* said? Althusser is a very clever man, but what he says about Marx is not Marx. Terms like 'essence' and 'dialectic' are Hegelian; infrastructure and superstructure are distinct."

"Are you friends with Althusser?" Cal inquired.

"Althusser has been for me a teacher and a guide, but I am convinced that Marx did not intend his works to be pored over by future generations. They were written in response to contemporary conditions and they were meant for immediate reaction."

"Compared to Sartre or Althusser, how do you perceive the role of the intellectual in society?" John asked.

"I now see the intellectual as something of a functionary. There are so many different types of intellectuals today. Some university intellectuals collaborate with business types, and there are other kinds of intellectuals who sit on committees dealing with community problems. The intellectual is a toolmaker, and he cannot dictate or even foreknow how the tools he creates will be used by the people.

Even in this respect the intellectual is not a prophet."

"So you reject the whole Leninist/Lukács notion of the avant-garde, the party intellectuals who perceive the truth the masses can't see," Cal concluded.

"Absolutely."

The fire petered out so Foucault suggested that he chop some wood. As he walked to the woodpile we could see him from the porch. David warned him about the large rattlesnakes that were around, but this did not deter Foucault in the slightest. After selecting some choice pieces, Foucault chopped the wood with great alacrity. Everybody unabashedly gawked in astonishment, as if to say, How is it that an esteemed Parisian intellectual can learn to chop wood with such dexterity? One could not imagine a Voltaire or Sartre accomplishing such a task so readily.

"But I am just an ordinary man," I heard Michel say to John, who had gone out to help him. Subsequently, the Bear Canyon band called him Country Joe Foucault, referring, I suppose, to his down-to-earth manner and skills.

I walked up to him while he was speaking to John about sexuality. "*Jouissance,*" he had just said softly.

"What did you say?" I blurted out tactlessly, revealing my pathetic understanding of spoken French.

"*Jouissance,*" Foucault shouted, piercing me with his glance. He was vexed, as if to say, How could you not know that word, of all words? The only other words I heard him use with such vigor were "*amour,*" "*savoir,*" and "*vérité.*"

AFTER ANOTHER HOUR in and around the residence, David took us on a hike above the cabin. We forded the stream and took a steep, narrow trail leading to a sun-drenched crest blanketed with cacti and sage. In the distance there was a colony of yucca plants.

"That yucca looks like a bouquet of serpents," I said.

"It looks like asparagus to me," Foucault observed with a laugh.

"When the yucca blooms, it sprouts a gigantic phallus covered with delicate flowers," I exclaimed to Foucault. "A forest of blooming yuccas is like the palace of sandstone cocks in Canyonlands, Utah. Michel, we will take you there for your next trip."

Foucault greeted the prospect with a broad smile and a firm assent.

David took the urge to climb a large Ponderosa pine.

Foucault was thrilled and circled the tree many times, shouting, "*Oh là là, oh là là*, David, you are very brave."

When David dismounted the last branch, Foucault said to him, "I love these mountains through you. You bring the mountains to me." To Cal he remarked, "Even a née-Marxist like yourself must like the mountains." Everyone laughed.

Cal took Foucault aside to engage him in conversation about psychology. We overheard Foucault say that our unconscious mind is shaped by and for others. To discern the nature of the unconscious we must listen to our discourse as well as to others.

After a quiet moment at the lookout gazing at the expansive San Antonio Canyon, which opens its massive thighs toward an embrace with the ocean crouching on the horizon, we made our way farther up the trail, which broadens considerably. Jake said that the massive exposed roots of the pines, which flowed down the sides of the mountain like a swarm of gigantic worms, always brought to his mind Sartre's idea of nausea and Kierkegaard's sickness unto death.

Foucault asked us why Americans are so obsessed with death. "There are so many books about death here," he observed. "In America the funeral home is a landmark, whereas in Europe undertakers are inconspicuous."

"Americans are so materialistic. They are compelled to think about the loss of their things," Jim answered.

"And egoistic, so the loss of self is a frightening prospect," Jake said.

"Religious mania is strong—the hunger for a better life in the hereafter," John offered.

"Have you seen *The Loved One*, the film based on Evelyn Waugh's novel about the ridiculous and garish Forest Lawn Cemetery in Los Angeles?" David asked.

"Oh, yes, I have," Foucault answered. "I liked it. It told me a lot about the American way of death. Perhaps we can drive by it and I will see you standing there in the nude," Foucault said with a grin, alluding to the replica of Michelangelo's sculpture at the entrance.

"Do you still uphold the concept of 'the death of man,' his 'visage washed away like a drawing in the sand on a beach'?" Jim asked. He told Foucault that he had taken *The Order of Things* in his backpack for an entire year, reading in it every chance he got.

"I think now that book ends on too pessimistic a note," Foucault answered. "I have since changed my outlook. I am more hopeful now, especially when I consider today's youth. Even in France the children are establishing new kinds of relationships with their families. I no longer believe that the face of man is being washed away. All that was much too apocalyptic anyway."

Cal told Michel that he felt he needed some kind of psychotherapy. He asked Michel what kind he would recommend. "What about Freudian?" he suggested.

Michel assented. "Freudian will be fine."

"Given the fact," I said, "that these days Cal, like so many of us, vacillates between revolutionary and clinical schizophrenia—" Foucault stopped me with a prolonged fit of laughter, as if he had not heard Deleuze's terms used in that fashion, so casually, "—I would have thought schizoanalysis would be more in order."

"There cannot be a general theory of psychoanalysis; everyone must do it for themselves," Foucault remarked.

THE POOL

We reached a pool in the rocks. While some of the men took off their hiking shorts and waded in the icy water, another group joined Foucault, who sat on a rock perched perilously over a waterfall. He admired a flock of blue jays that had found us cavorting in the stream and now sat staring impatiently from the trees hoping for human food.

David admonished Michel, "Don't admire the jays. They have learned to imitate all the other birdcalls. With this weapon these predators are able to interfere with the breeding and nursing patterns of all the other birds. They are taking over the forest."

"Yes, the jays remind me of certain groups of people," Chris said.

Foucault listened intently and shifted closer to David.

After a little while I started up the conversation yet again, much to Foucault's chagrin. "Have you met Klossowski? I am very much taken with his idea of 'creative chaos,' the theme he uses to conclude his book on Nietzsche."

"Oh, yes. I have great esteem for Klossowski. What a remarkable family—Rilke was his half-brother, and Balthus, the artist..." Foucault stopped. He had assumed a serious, almost reverential tone of voice, indicating a deep respect for the knowledge generated by his peers.

Foucault resumed speaking to David about such matters for a few minutes. Then David engaged Michel on more intimate terms, which was an endearing charm he possessed. He turned his deep-set, inquiring, troubled eyes to him and said: "Michel, are you happy?"

"I am happy with my life, not so much with myself," Michel perked up.

"In other words, you don't feel proud of yourself, but you are happy with the way your life has taken shape and is unfolding."

"Yes."

"But it seems to me that it is hard to make such a distinction. If you like the way your life has developed and you feel some sort of responsibility for it, then it seems you probably would feel good about yourself too."

"Well, I don't feel responsible for what's happened to me in my life."

"But don't you think that Nietzsche believed that it is important to try to feel *the will* that you have within yourself as a person?"

"No, I don't think Nietzsche was saying that. Nietzsche was using the power of the individual man as an instrument to combat the moral order that had been established, but he does not belong in any way to the tradition of individualism, which establishes the individual man as the important one in the historical context."

"In fact," Foucault continued uninterrupted, "Nietzsche was saying how little a man is responsible for his nature, especially in terms of what he considered to be his morality. Morality has been constitutive of the individual's being. The individual is contingent, formed by the weight of moral tradition, not really autonomous."

"What effect do you think Nietzsche's health had on him? Is it notable that he went mad given his intellectual position—that 'creative chaos' Simeon just mentioned?"

"There are two aspects to consider with regard to Nietzsche's health. One is that he was very sick and his body was failing him. He was very ill. You just have to consider his life in those terms. Of course, there is Nietzsche's madness. But..." Foucault broke off in exasperation.

I intervened by asking Foucault when Nietzsche's work, which I knew he was editing in a complete French translation, had made its great impact upon him.

"I read some Nietzsche when I was studying philosophy in Paris, but it was not until I returned to Paris from Sweden in 1959 that I *really* read Nietzsche. I have since been puzzled by the fact that he did not mean that much to me when I was a philosophy student."

"It seems to me, Michel," David interjected, "that you are Nietzschean in the sense that you follow his motto 'Live dangerously.'"

Foucault laughed and said, "Why do you say that?"

"Well, what about the Death Valley trip?" David proposed, furrowing his brow.

"Oh, that was no risk. I had Simeon and Michael with me," Foucault said with an ironic expression, as if to agree with David's assessment of his risk-taking nature.

"What did you think about on your trip?"

"One thing it brought home to me was the reason I love Malcolm

Lowry so much. I saw that Lowry had a hallucinogenic experience on alcohol. He used it as a vision, a Truth experience."

"Do you like cocaine?" John asked, clearing his sinuses.

"Not really. I find it is anti-aphrodisiac."

Lance wondered aloud if Foucault liked the men in Brazil.

"A lot," he said. "I have a lover in Brazil."

"How did you meet him?"

"I was walking alone on the beach and he passed by me. He smiled directly at me. That's all it took. What I particularly like about Brazil, and California for that matter, is that the boys are not proud or arrogant. As opposed to Europe, the boys don't strut around; they are at ease with their bodies. They are accessible. A bit like ancient Greece."

"Why do you think the boys in Brazil are so accessible?" Lance continued.

"Maybe it is because so many of them are poor," Foucault responded.

WE LEFT THE POOL and hiked a little farther to Bear Flats, a lush meadow encapsulated by the flanks of Mount Baldy. I took some photographs with my Leica while Foucault ambled with Lance among the jade-green leaves of a manzanita garden. They were discussing the young men of Morocco. When they returned I broke the sad news that it was time to go back down the mountain and return to that infernal oxymoron, the smog-infested Claremont.

On the trail Michel sometimes walked alone, but more often he was accompanied by one or more of the young men. They all could not get enough of each other's company.

When we reached the last escarpment, Lance and I talked to Foucault as we descended a perilous wooden staircase reminiscent of one in a Tarzan movie. "Do you like to go to see films, Michel?" I asked.

"Yes. But I miss a lot of them. A film usually stays in Paris about a month. I'll go out of town, and when I come back, the film is gone."

"Who are some of your favorite filmmakers?"

"Fellini, Antonioni, Polanski. I liked *Chinatown* very much."

"No American filmmakers in your list?"

"Well, I guess it is stupid of me not to mention American filmmakers among my favorites," Foucault said. "But it is difficult for me to appreciate American films because they are so much determined by the big production aspects of Hollywood. If I don't grasp the director's techniques and how they work in a film, it is difficult for me to know exactly what the director is trying to say, particularly when he is working in and around these sorts of large productions."

"Do any American directors come to mind?" David inquired as he joined us for the last stretch of the trail.

"Hitchcock. I saw *Psycho* recently and liked it a lot. It's baroque. I would see it again. And *Vertigo* too."

Foucault turned to David and said, "Why don't you tell me some more about yourself?"

"Really, I don't want to talk about myself," David fired back, "but

I find it impossible not to. I feel I shouldn't. You, Michel, are so self-effacing, while I feel that I am caught up in a vicious cycle of self-manifestation. I have studied phenomenology to try to understand what is going on in me."

"But phenomenology has become so stylized," Foucault exclaimed. "It is not really getting to the heart of man's *empirical* situation. The phenomenologists are preventing mankind from asking the real questions about his existence. Still, phenomenological questions are important, I guess. One has to go through them."

"Then you don't think I am being too self-absorbed?" David exclaimed.

"It does not do any good to worry about being too much *into* yourself; that just intensifies the self-introspection," Foucault replied. "If that's what your mind is doing at a certain point and time, just let it do it. It's not something you should try to alter."

"I feel sometimes that I should just forget all about these questions about myself," David went on to say. "It is a waste of time and energy, self-defeating in a way."

"On the contrary, you should work through these subjective questions, especially in your youth," Foucault commented. "A person who has done so is going to be in better psychological shape in his thirties and thereafter. If people do not go through these passing psychological crises when they're younger, they will have problems in their thirties and thereafter."

"I am impressed with how sociable you are, Michel," Lance observed.

"No, I am not in fact sociable at all," Foucault confessed. "I try not to go to social events. But I feel awful when I hurt people's feelings. Recently I was driven down to Stanford University by some students. I was to give a lecture there. The students disclosed that lunch for me had been planned at the faculty club. I told them that I despise faculty clubs and formal lunches with the mandarins. The students told some faculty members what I had said and the lunch was summarily canceled. I felt terrible."

"Did you like the Stanford faculty?" John asked.

"Not at all. They are incredibly stuffy."

"When you lecture you seem to enjoy it," John continued.

"I lecture well when I feel well," Foucault admitted. "I feel happy with people in certain situations. Usually not before large numbers of people. Before I have to lecture, that is to say to work, I cannot even eat."

"Why are you so put off by large groups who come to listen to you?" John persisted.

"I don't think they can be serious," Foucault replied. "If you have too many people, it's not going to be possible for it to be serious. You have to be able to establish contact for there to be genuine communication and seriousness about what is happening, what is being said."

"What about the large gatherings of students in Paris during May '68? Were not they serious?" Cal butted in.

"That's different," Foucault admonished him. "In France, the theatricality of the demonstrators, their rowdiness, was a sign of their commitment, their seriousness, their aggression against the system."

"Did the events of May '68 have a great effect on you?" Jim inquired.

"Decisive!" was the reply. "It made my work possible. I am very impressed with the sixties as a phenomenon. I think the revolution initiated at that time is still going on, but in a much quieter way."

"I cannot understand the appeal of Maoism to the French left," Cal remarked. "The Chinese way cannot apply to the West."

Foucault agreed. "It cannot. The Chinese are stylized in their approach to things."

"I read recently that the French Communist Party has just come out against the Chinese regime," Cal continued.

"I am not surprised," Foucault remarked. "The French Communist Party is still heavily under the influence of the Soviets."

David abruptly turned to Foucault and said, "I am really put off by academic psychology and behaviorism."

"It amounts to the same thing as making a distinction between clinical psychology and psychiatry," Foucault commented. "Psychology with its emphasis on testing, psychiatry with its..."

The dialogue broke off then because we had reached the parking lot at the foot of the canyon. Michel graciously bid farewell to the party of young men. As we got into the car I was compelled to say, "Michel, there are so many of us here who love you. You must sense that we are so grateful for your work and the enlightenment you have brought to us."

He was taken aback and looked at me with disbelief. But he thanked me modestly.

THE FOUNDERS ROOM

At the late lunch with some faculty at the Claremont Men's College, Foucault, glowing with the warmth and serenity of Bear Canyon, was expansive and charming. A female history professor made an effort to converse with him about her speciality, early nineteenth-century American military history. Finally, she gave up and, unable to discuss anything else, asked him what he thought of his trip to Death Valley.

He replied, "It was the greatest experience of my life."

After lunch I took Foucault to my office at the Claremont Graduate School. I explained to him that, during my first few years here, when it got too cold in the mountains David and I, along with our dogs, would sleep in my office. We were too poor to afford an apartment. One morning we overslept and the secretary discovered us dishabille on the office floor. Foucault laughed a lot at that story.

I showed him the recently completed manuscript of my book, *Luxury and Restraint in the Enlightenment.* He expressed approval but nothing more.

I produced a copy of a piece I had just written called "The Early Foucault." He looked at the manuscript and smiled but did not even read the first sentence.

"When I say something," he said, with his steely eyes directed right at me, "I am speaking to the present. What I say is not intended to speak to the future, at least in the sense that it will necessarily apply to the future or that I can know how it will be used in the future."

The last official duty he had to confront was a discussion with my class in the Founders Room. Michel beamed as he walked into the fine paneled hall. One could see that he was very pleased with the character and responsiveness of the assembled group of young men and women. By all appearances it was the kind of company he liked to keep.

He sat cross-legged on top of the desk and began to entertain questions, which he answered with the flair of a Gielgud. The Death Valley trip and the Bear Canyon trail seem to have made him even more outgoing, his public speaking even more polished. He generously spoke in English and sustained that incomparable charm he possessed, that chiseled quality of clear expression. One of the students happened to audiotape the dialogue. Toni Tosch, a skillful secretary in Claremont, did a splendid job of transcribing it. I have edited it slightly to make the English syntax more fluent.

☽ ✿ ☾

Student: I want to ask about the relation between discourse and power. If discourse is the center for some independent power, the source of power—if "source" is the right word—how are we to find that source? What is the difference between what you are doing in your analysis of discourse and what the traditional phenomenological method seeks to do?

Foucault: I do not want to try to find behind the discourse something which would be the power and which would be the source of the discourse as in a phenomenological description or any method of interpretation. We start from the discourse *as it is!* In a phenomenological description you try to find out from discourse something about the speaking subject; you try to find the intentions of the thinking thought of the speaking subject from the discourse.

The kind of analysis I make does not deal with the problem of the speaking subject but looks at the ways in which the discourse plays a role inside the strategical system in which power is involved, for which power is working. So power won't be something outside the discourse. Power won't be something like a source or the origin of discourse. Power will be something which is working through the discourse, since the discourse is itself a piece of a strategical system of power relations. Is that clear?

☽ ✧ ☾

Student: Suppose you write about such a system of discourse. Does the text that you write capture the power? Does it replicate or repeat the power? Would those be the words? Or would you want to say that it intends the power or meaning—or should we say "has the power as its meaning"?

Foucault: No, the power is not the meaning of the discourse.

The discourse is a series of elements which works inside the general mechanism of power. So, you have to take the discourse as a series of events, such as political events through which power is conveyed and conducted.

☾ ✧ ☽

Student: I'm concerned about the historian's text. What, in fact, does the historian say about the discourse of the past? What is the relation between power and the historian's text?

Foucault: I do not understand exactly why you speak of the discourse of historians. But may I take another example which for me is more familiar?

The problem of madness, of discourse about madness, and what has been said in certain periods about madness: I do not think the problem is to know who noted this discourse, what was the way of thinking or even perceiving madness in the consciousness of people during a particular period, but to look at the discourse about madness, the institutions about madness, the way in which people were excluded since they had no jobs or since they were homosexual, etc.

All these elements belong to a system of power in which discourse is only a piece related to others. Elements which are partnerships. The analysis consists in describing the relations and the reciprocal relations between all those elements. Is that clearer?

Student: Thank you.

☽ ☿ ☾

Student: Last night you mentioned that you have just finished a book on penal reform and legal systems, [and] the type of exclusion that has operated in that framework. I'm interested in knowing if you can develop a model of power in terms of the prison system. How do you see what is being done to prisoners? Is it punishment and rehabilitation?

Foucault: Well, I think that I have found the figure for this kind of power, of this system of power. I've found it very well described in Bentham's Panopticon. We can describe very generally the system of exclusion of madness in the seventeenth and eighteenth centuries. At the end of the eighteenth century, society brought forth a mode of power which was not based on *exclusion,* as we still say, but *inclusion* inside the system in which everybody should be located, surveyed, observed during night and day, in which everybody would be linked to his own identity.

You know that Jeremy Bentham has dreamed of the perfect prison—well, of the kind of building which could be either a hospital or a prison or an asylum or a school or a factory—in which there will be a central tower with windows all around. Then a space with nothing in it and another building with cells all around and with windows here, and here, and here. [Foucault proceeded to sketch on the blackboard an illustration of Bentham's model prison.]

In each of these cells there will be either a worker or a madman or a schoolboy or a prisoner. You need only one man located here in the central tower to observe exactly what they are doing all the time in these small cells. In Bentham, that's the real ideal for all those guys in institutions. In Bentham I have found the Columbus of politics. I think one finds in the Panopticon a kind of mytho-logical motif of the new kind of power system our society uses nowadays.

$$) \; ✩ \; ($$

Student: Do you consider yourself a philosopher or a historian?

Foucault: Neither.

Student: But isn't history the major subject of your work? What is the basis of your notion of history?

Foucault: My program has been an analysis of discourse, but not with the perspective of the "point of view." Nor is my program grounded in the methods of linguistics. The notion of structure has no meaning for me. What interests me in the problem of discourse is the fact that somebody has said something at one moment.

I do not wish to stress the meaning but the function of the fact that this thing has been spoken by somebody at this point. That is what I call the "event." For me, the problem is to take dis-course as a series of events and to make relations and to describe relationships between these events, which we can call discursive events, with the other events in the economic system or in the political field or institutions and so on.

Discourse from this point of view is nothing more than an event like the others, but of course discursive events have spe-cific functions among other events. A similar problem is to note what constitutes the specific functions of discourse and to look at particular kinds of discourse among other ones. I also study the strategical functions of particular kinds of discursive events in a political system or in a power system. Is that enough?

) ☾ (

Student: How would you describe your vision of history? How does the dimension of history come into discourse?

Foucault: Since I consider discourse as a *series* of events, we are automatically in the dimension of history. The problem is that for fifty years most historians have chosen to study and describe not events but structures. There is now a kind of coming back to events in the field of history.

What I mean is that in the nineteenth century what historians called an event was a battle, a victory, the death of a king, or something like that. Against this kind of history, the historians of colonies or societies, and so on, have shown that in history there have been a lot of permanent structures. The task of the historian was to make these structures clear. We can see that aim in France in the work of Lucien Febvre, Marc Bloch, and so on. Now, historians are returning to the events and trying to note the way we can speak of economic evolution or demographic evolution as an event.

As an example, I will take a point which has been studied for many years now: The operation of birth control in the sexual life of Western society is still very enigmatic. This phenomenon is a very important event from the standpoint of economics and from the biological point of view. We know that birth control has been practiced in England and France for many centuries. Of course, the practice of birth control occurred mostly among small, aristocratic circles, but it also occurred among very poor people. We know now that in the South of France and in the countryside birth control has been practiced systematically since the second half of the eighteenth century. That's an event.

Let's take another example: Since a particular time in the nineteenth century the rate of protein in food has been growing and the rate of the gristle has been diminishing. This constitutes a historical, economic, biological event. The historian is now engaged in studying these processes as new *kinds* of events. I think that this is something people like me have in common with historians. I am not a historian in the strict sense. But we share an interest in the event.

☽☼☾

Student: What in this new type of historical inquiry is the place of what you call the archaeology of knowledge? Does your use of the phrase "archaeology of knowledge" refer to a new type of methodology or is it a simple analogy between the techniques of archaeology and history?

Foucault: Let me backtrack for a moment and add something to what I was saying about the event as the main object of research. Neither the logic of meaning nor the logic of structure are pertinent for this kind of research. We don't need the theory and logic of meaning, we don't need the logic or method of structure; we need something else.

Student: I understand. Now would you comment on whether the archaeology of knowledge is a new method or simply a metaphor?

Foucault: Well...

Student: Is it central to your conception of history?

Foucault: I use the word "archaeology" for two or three main reasons. The first is that we can play with the word "archaeology." *"Arche"* in Greek means "beginning." We also use the word *"l'arche"* in French. The French signifies the way in which discursive events have been registered and can be extracted from the archive. So "archaeology" refers to the kind of research which tries to dig out discursive events as if they were registered in an *arche*.

The second reason I use the term relates to a particular aim of mine. I wish to reconstitute a historical field in its totality, with all the political, economic, and sexual connections, and so on. My problem is to find out what to analyze, what has been the fact itself of discourse. In this way I don't intend to be a historian but to know why and in what ways connections occur between discursive events. If I do this it is because I would like to know just what we are *now*, nowadays. I wish to focus on what is happening with us today, what are we, what is our society. I think that our society and what we are has a deep historical dimension, and in this historical space the discursive events which have taken place centuries ago, or years ago, are very important. We are interwoven into those discursive events. In a way we are nothing else but what has been said, centuries and months and weeks ago, and so on.

☽ ☼ ☾

Student: It seems to me that any theory of power, whether it's based on structures or functions, always implies a qualitative feature. If you're going to study the structure and function of power events in a particular society—for instance, Franco's Spain or Mao's People's Republic—you have qualitatively different structures and uses of power. In that sense I think any theory of power has to address itself to its ideological underpinnings. In that sense it's very difficult to establish the kind of events or explanations about the structure or function of power apart from their political connotations. Therefore you see it's ideologically not free.

Foucault: I cannot say anything more than I agree.

Student: But if you agree, don't you think this is a serious limitation on the attempt to construct a paradigm of power which is based on one's political convictions?

Foucault: That's the reason why I don't intend to depict a paradigm of what power is. I would like to note the ways different mechanisms of power are at work in our society, among us, inside us, outside us. I would like to know the ways in which our bodies, our daily behavior, our sexual behavior, our desire, our scientific and theoretical discourses are linked with several systems of power, which are themselves linked each with one another.

Student: How would your position be different from a person who had adopted a materialist interpretation of history?

Foucault: I think that the difference is that in historical materialism you have to locate at the base of the system the political forces, then the relations of production and so on, until you find the structure, the juridical and ideological superstructure, and finally what will deepen our own thinking as well as the consciousness of poor people.

I think that power relations are simpler, but at the same time much more complicated—simple in the sense that you do not need these pyramidal constructions, much more complicated in the sense that you have a lot of reciprocal relations between, for instance, the technology of power and the development of productive forces.

You cannot understand the development of productive forces unless you perceive in industry and society a particular kind of several types of power at work—that is to say, at work inside the productive forces. The human body is a productive force, we know that, but the human body does not exist like *that*, like a biological article, like a piece of material. The human body is something which exists in and through a political system. Political power gives you some room, room to behave, to have a particular attitude, to sit in a certain way, to work the whole day long, and so on.

Marx thought, and he has written, that work constitutes the concrete existence of man. I think *that* is a typical Hegelian idea. Work is not the concrete essence of man. If man works, if the human body is a productive force, it is because man is obliged to work. He is obliged to work because he is invested by political forces, because he is inserted into power mechanisms, and so forth.

Student: Really what bothers me is how does this position falsify the basic Marxian premise? Marx thought that if people are obliged to work we are therefore obliged to enter into some kind of socialization to carry out that process of production. As a consequence of this we have what is called structural relationships.

If one is to understand the kinds of social relations which exist in a particular society, one has to investigate the kinds of power structures which are linked to the processes of production. And I don't think it's a determinate relationship. I mean, I really think it's a reciprocal relationship, a dialectical relationship.

Foucault: I don't accept this word "dialectical." No. No! Let me make this very clear. As soon as you say "dialectical" you begin to accept, even if you don't say it, the Hegelian schema of thesis/ antithesis and a kind of logic that I think is inadequate for making a real concrete description of those problems. A reciprocal relation is not a dialectical one.

Student: But if you only accept the idea of "reciprocal" to describe these relationships, you take away any kind of contradiction. That's why I think the use of the word "dialectical" is important.

Foucault: Well, let's examine the word "contradiction." But first let me say that I am glad you have asked this question. I think it's very important. You see, the word "contradiction" has a particular meaning in the field of logic. In the logic of propositions, you really know what contradiction is. But when you look at reality and seek to describe and analyze a lot of processes, you find that those zones of reality don't contain any contradiction.

Look at the biological field. You find a lot of antagonistic reciprocal processes, but this does not mean you have found contradictions. This does not mean that one side of the antagonistic process is positive and the other negative. I think that it is really important to understand that struggle; antagonistic processes and so on do not mean contradiction in the logical sense, as the dialectical point of view presupposes. There is no dialectic in nature. I beg to differ from Engels, but in nature—and Darwin has shown it very well—there are a lot of antagonistic processes. But they are not dialectical. I think that this sort of Hegelian formulation will not hold water.

If I continually insist that there are such processes as struggle, fight, antagonistic mechanisms, etc., it is because you find these processes in reality. They are not dialectical ones. Nietzsche spoke a lot about those processes, and even more often than Hegel. But Nietzsche described these antagonisms without reference to dialectical relations.

Student: Can we apply this to a specific concrete situation? If one considers the subject of work in industrial society, let us say, in relation to a worker's specific problem, is this relationship reciprocal or antagonistic or what? If I analyze my own problems in this society, do I see them as reciprocal relationships or as antagonistic relationships?

Foucault: It is neither one nor the other. Now you are invoking the problem of alienation. But you see, there are a lot of things we can say about alienation. When you say "my problems," don't you bring in the major philosophical, the main theoretical questions—for example, what is property, what is the human subject? You said "*my* problems." Well, that would be another discussion.

The fact that you have work and that the product of work, of your work, belongs to somebody else, that's something. It's not contradiction, it's not a reciprocal combination, it's a matter of a fight, a struggle. Anyway, the fact that what you have been working at belongs to somebody else does not take on a dialectical shape. This does not constitute a contradiction. You might believe that it is morally indefensible, that you cannot bear it, that you have to struggle against this fact, yes, that's it. But this is not a contradiction, it is not a logical contradiction. And, I think that dialectical logic is really very poor; it's very easy to use it, but it's really very poor if you want to formulate very precise meanings, descriptions, and analyses of power processes.

) ☼ (

Student: What, if any, normative concerns underlie your research?

Foucault: Is that not a question that we spoke about yesterday evening, when somebody asked me what we should do now?

Student: Well, no. For example, your choice of subjects. What leads you to that choice instead of another?

Foucault: Well, that is very difficult to answer. I could answer on a personal level, I could answer on a conjectural level, or I could try to answer on a theoretical level. I will concentrate on the second one, the conjectural.

I had a discussion with somebody yesterday evening. He said, "You are working in such fields as madness, penal systems, etc., but all this has nothing to do with politics."

Well, I think he was right from a traditional Marxist point of view. This means that, during the sixties, problems like psychiatry or sexuality were considered quite marginal when they were compared to the great political problems—the exploitation of workers, for example.

Among the leftists in France and in Europe, no one at that time looked at such problems as psychiatry and sexuality, because they were considered marginal and unimportant. But I think that, since destalinization since the sixties, we have discovered that a lot of things that we thought of as unimportant and marginal are really very central in the political field, because political power does not lie only in the great institutional forms of the state, what we call the state apparatus.

There is no single place in which power is at work, but many places: in the family, in sexual life, in the way mad people are treated, in the exclusion of homosexuals, in the relations between men and women, and so on. These are all political relations. If we want to change society, we cannot do it without changing these relations.

The example of the Soviet Union has been decisive. The Soviet Union is a country in which we can say that since the Revolution the relations of production have changed. The legal system of property was changed. Also the political. Institutions have been changed since the Revolution. But all these small and very minute power relations in the family, in sexuality, in the factory, among the workers, etc.—all those relations are still in the Soviet Union what they are in other Western countries. Nothing has *really* changed.

☽ ☿ ☾

Student: In your recent work on the penal code and the penal system, you refer to the importance of Bentham's Panopticon. In your *Discourse on Language* you stated that you were going to examine the effects of psychiatric discourse on the penal code. Now I'm wondering whether you consider Bentham's model prison part of psychiatric discourse or whether you just consider it evidence relating to the way psychiatric discourse influenced the penal code?

Foucault: I would say the second. That is, I think that Bentham has given this kind of issue not only a figure but also a text. It was really for him a new technology of power that could be applied to mental illness as well as much else besides.

Student: Do you think then that Bentham's specific work exerted an influence on its own, or was it just representative of general influences on scientific discourse?

Foucault: Of course Bentham had a huge influence, and you

can really discern the effect of his direct influence. For instance, the way in which the prisons have been built and administered in Europe and in the States is derived directly from Bentham.

In the beginning of the twentieth century in the USA—but I do not remember where—a particular prison was considered a wonderful model, with certain minor modifications, for a mental hospital. If it has been the case that such a dream as Bentham's Panopticon, that such a paranoiac has exerted such enormous influence, it was because at the same moment a new technology of power was being built up in all society. For instance, the new system of surveillance in the army, in the school—the way in which children were placed under surveillance every day by the teacher—and on and on, all this was happening at the same time, and the whole process can be found in the paranoiac dream of Bentham. It is the paranoiac dream of our society, the *paranoiac truth* of our society.

☽ ✧ ☾

Student: Getting back to reciprocal influences and your dis-illusionment with the attention that has been directed to the speaking subject, would it be incorrect to single out Bentham? Was not Bentham influenced by the practices of the schools, the army surveillance, etc., at the time? Should we not say that it is improper to focus on Bentham per se, and to direct our attention to all these influences radiating from the society?

Foucault: Yes.

) ☼ (

Student: You said that we are obliged to work. Do we want to work? Do we choose to work?

Foucault: Yes, we desire to work, we want to work, we love to work, but work is not our essence. To say that we want to work is very different from defining our *essence* in terms of our desire to work. Marx said that work is the essence of man. This conception is essentially Hegelian. It is very difficult to integrate it into the class struggle in the nineteenth century.

You might know that Lafargue, the son-in-law of Marx, wrote a small book which nobody speaks about in Marxist circles. The neglect of Lafargue's book amuses me. The indifference to it is ironic, but, more than ironic, it is symptomatic! He has written a book in the nineteenth century on man's love of leisure. For him, it was really impossible to imagine that work is the essence of man. Between man and work there is no essential relation.

Student: It's something that we do.

Foucault: What's that?

Student: Work!

Foucault: Sometimes.

) ☼ (

Student: Would you clarify the rapport between madness and the artist? Perhaps with reference to Artaud. How can we relate

Artaud the madman to Artaud the artist, if we can or should?

Foucault: Really, I cannot answer this question. I would say that the single question that concerns me is why is it possible that, from the end of the eighteenth century to the present day, madness has been for us and continues to be something related to genius, beauty, art, and so on? Why do we have this curious idea that if somebody is a great artist then there must be something mad about him?

We could say the same about crime. When somebody makes something like a very beautiful crime, people don't think he might be something of a genius, that there might be madness at work. The relation between madness and crime and beauty and art, and so on, is very enigmatic. I think that we have to try to understand why we think of these relations as something very evident. But I don't like to treat these questions directly—questions such as Are artists mad, or In what way are artists or criminals mad? The assumption that these relations are evident persists in our society. We treat these relations as cultural and very typical.

☽ ☆ ☾

Student: Last night you called Sartre the last prophet. You suggested that the task for the intellectual now is to develop the tools and techniques for analysis, to understand the various ways in which power manifests itself. Are you not a prophet? Don't you predict events or the ways in which your ideas will be used?

Foucault: I am a journalist. I am interested in the present. I use history to understand what is happening to us now.

Student: Then you are saying that what is done with the tools and the disclosures which intellectuals make is not their province. Are you suggesting that the problem of what to do with the work of the intellectuals belongs to the workers, to the people? Can you anticipate the ways in which your tools and analyses might be put to use? Can you foresee ways they might be used which you would not condone?

Foucault: No, I cannot anticipate. What I would say is that I think that we have to be very modest about the eventual political use of what we are saying and what we are doing. I do not think there is such a thing as a conservative philosophy or a revolutionary philosophy. Revolution is a political process; it is an economic process. Revolution is not a philosophical ideology. And that's important. That's the reason why something like Hegelian philosophy has been a revolutionary ideology, a revolutionary method, and a revolutionary tool, but *also* a conservative one.

Look at Nietzsche. Nietzsche brought forth wonderful ideas, or tools, if you like. He was used by the Nazi Party. Now a lot of leftist thinkers use him. So we cannot be sure if what we are saying is revolutionary or not.

This is, I think, the first thing we have to recognize. It doesn't mean that we are simply to make very beautiful, or useful, or funny tools and then choose which ones to put on the market in case somebody wants to buy them or use them.

All that is fine, but there is more to it than that. If you are trying to do something—for example, to make an analysis or formulate a theory—you have to know clearly how you want it to be used, for what purposes you want to make use of the tool you're building up—*you*—and how you want your tools to relate to the others which are being fashioned just now. So that I think the relation between the present conjunctive situation and what you are doing within a theoretical framework is really important. You have to make these relations very clear in your own mind. You cannot make tools for *any* purpose, you have to make them for *one* purpose, but you have to realize that maybe those tools will be used in other ways.

The ideal is not to build tools but to make bombs, because when you have used up your own bombs, nobody else can use them. And I must add that my dream, my personal dream, is not exactly to build bombs, because I don't like to kill people. I would like to write book-bombs—that means books that are useful just at the moment in which they are written or read by people. Then they would disappear. Books would be such that they would disappear soon after they have been read or used. Books should be a kind of bomb and nothing else. After the explosion, people could be reminded that the books made a very beautiful fireworks display. In later years historians and others could recount that such and such a book was useful as a bomb and was beautiful as fireworks.

Well, I want to thank you very much. I have been very glad to be here and to hear and answer your questions. I have been very interested and impressed by all that you have said and what you know about my poor work. I feel that I don't deserve the attention, but I am grateful you know so much. Anyway, I would really like to meet you again.

IMMEDIATELY AFTER THE DISCUSSION a comparative literature professor rushed up and asked Foucault to make a further comment about Artaud.

"I cannot," Foucault replied. "You see I am not really interested in literature."

Meanwhile, a professor of American government sidled up and professed to Foucault that he only wished he could teach some new ideas about criminology, but such a bold step was unthinkable. After all, what would his colleagues think, not to mention the administration. He would lose grants and prestige.

Before Foucault could respond to his imbecility, I spotted a powerful satrap, an American history professor. I graciously introduced Foucault to him, but His Eminence did not even acknowledge the introduction. Standing before the distinguished visitor from France, he just looked vacant and walked on. I was astonished at his incivility. I knew that he was obsessed with America, and on his only trip out of the country, a visit to Paris, he had proudly announced that he had fled back to the United States after two days because he missed his native land so much. I suspect that xenophobia coupled with homophobia was behind his rude response to Michel Foucault.

Then an English professor, whose manner was something of a

cross between King George III and the Baron de Charlus, lumbered across the lawn, cornered Foucault, and demanded to know what he thought of Virginia Woolf.

Foucault, a bit harrowed, exclaimed, "No more questions!"

SAMBO'S

It was a great relief to get away from the academicians. We joined up with Mike and David. Foucault had only a few hours to catch his plane. On our way to the Ontario Airport we took Foucault to Sambo's, a coffee shop on Foothill at the San Bernardino Freeway entrance. It was decorated with scenes from a popular story about the jungle adventures of a group of black children. There were subtle, malicious racist overtones to the decor.

"Since it is the most anonymous coffee shop in town," I explained, "I took refuge here a few years ago when David and I were not getting along. I drank coffee and read Proust."

"A perfect place for reading Proust," Foucault commented. "Balbec!" Foucault's wicked analogy between the tacky restaurant and the bourgeois resort, which figures so prominently in Proust's seven-volume novel, made my head spin. In that one similitude, Foucault made me grasp the nature of the bourgeoisie in a totally new way.

Foucault ordered a turkey sandwich and a glass of iced tea.

"What would you do if you were caught at the Paris airport with marijuana in your luggage?" David inquired.

"I would make a statement to the people of France telling them that marijuana, hashish, and similar drugs should be decriminalized," Foucault answered. "I would point out the absurdity of imprisoning boys who are caught with two grams of marijuana while the culture promotes alcohol."

Foucault suddenly craned his neck to observe something going on at the entrance to the coffee shop. "Look at that new Mercedes just arriving," he remarked. "That you would not see in Europe. No one who drives that kind of car in Europe would come to eat at a place like this." He continued, "David, would you like to have a car like that?"

"No, I would rather have a Porsche. But then, I had a Porsche and sold it because I felt bad about having a luxury car."

"Oh, you made an *ethical* decision, then," Foucault said emphatically.

"I guess you could call it that."

"What kind of car do you have, Michel?" Mike inquired.

"I have a very used Renault," he responded sheepishly.

WE FELL SILENT while we ate our sandwiches. After a while Foucault started up another round of conversation.

"Look at the diners," Foucault observed. "They are all dressed alike, talking about the same things in the same manner, eating the same kinds of food. Why is there so much *sameness* in America? The consumption patterns in America are so limited, so homogeneous."

"Is there anywhere you see difference in America?" Mike asked.

"Yes, the universities. If you do not spend time in the universities you would think everyone in America is the same. At least if a college student were dining here he would likely be wearing clothes that would set him apart. He wouldn't blend in."

"The universities in California are on the defensive," I said, "as indeed are all the human services since Ronald Reagan has been governor of the state."

"Yes, I know about Reagan and the political changeover he represents," Foucault acknowledged. "What is going on in the universities is very mysterious to me now. Whatever it is, it is happening all over the world. I feel that a close involvement with Berkeley, out of all the places, will allow me to identify exactly what is happening in the universities everywhere."

The coffee shop was located in full view of a fire station, which prompted Foucault to say, "I have noticed that in America there are so many fire stations. The major myth in America is fire, but in California it is earthquake. Americans really cling to their myths."

"The earthquake myth is so strong here that some people think California will break off into the Pacific Ocean," Mike said.

"California would not sink, so it would not be a disaster," Foucault went on to say. On the contrary, California would become an island and begin floating toward China. It would take thousands of years before it got to China, but it would just be floating along and the people of California would be on it, doing their thing, separated, in a very physical and geographic sense, from the rest of the United States and the whole Western world."

"Don't you think the Golden Gate Bridge looks to the East in the same way the Statue of Liberty faces Europe, the Old World?" Mike now asked. "That the Bridge and the Statue face in opposite directions, the Bridge is the end whereas the Statue is the beginning?"

"The Golden Gate Bridge should be understood symbolically," Foucault responded, "in the sense that it does not go from America back to America but that it should be something that could possibly open up out of America."

"Do you think Americans are just too open and outgoing for their own good? Do Europeans still make fun of Americans on this count?" David asked.

Foucault replied, "Yes, I have heard Europeans scoff at American friendliness, the American way of 'being nice,' but they are mistaken. We spend a lot of time with strangers, so why not enjoy it? We probably spend at least three-fourths of our time in very short encounters with people, in chance encounters. This way of relating to people, then, is very important. Why buy hostility with your groceries? Be friendly with the checker and the stock clerk! Antagonism against each other only saps the energy that could and should be directed against the systems of power that oppress us."

"Norman Mailer spoke in Claremont the other night," David said, "and Simeon accused him of glorifying aggression, particularly male aggression against women. Do you think aggression is natural?"

"I am not willing to challenge the naturalists on this point," Foucault stated. "But that does not mean we cannot control aggression, channel it toward the right things—not toward each other but toward the system that dominates us. We should eliminate aggression when it interferes with the intimate contact that should exist between people."

DEPARTURE

On the way to the airport, Foucault said, "Los Angeles has such wealth, such amazing affluence. The architecture is remarkable. And there is the immense size. Paris is so much more limited. You can walk across Paris in two hours." Is there an artist's colony here—young artists, I mean to say?"

"Yes, in Venice and Santa Monica there are a lot of young artists," Michael replied.

"Do you like to cook?" David asked.

"Yes, I do. Why don't you spend some time with me in Paris? I would love to cook for you," Foucault said.

"Maybe," David replied.

"Michel," I implored him, "Michael and I have only been together for a half year now, but I am still distressed about something. Perhaps your experience can help."

"What's bothering you?"

"Well, it's kind of banal, but I feel so lonely and rejected when Michael goes out on a date with someone else. I guess I am too possessive."

"Then you find someone else to go out with," he responded.

"Are you suggesting a kind of open contract between us?"

"Not a contract. The notion of contract is a residue from Rome," Michel said. "Why imitate marriage?"

"But can't I expect reciprocity in this relationship?" I asked.

"No, not in the sense of 'you give me this and I'll give you the equivalent.'"

"Then what kind of reciprocity?"

"Asymmetrical. Don't expect to receive what you give."

"Sometimes old-fashioned coupling seems so desirable in a cozy sort of way."

"Why? You have the key to happiness."

"How is that?"

"You are free. You can be open to a variety of intense relationships that enrich each other."

"How does this relate to the sense of obligation we have toward each other?"

"From the center of obligation, relationships should develop in many different directions."

"Is this the way you live?"

"I try to! When we lived together, the biggest problem my lover and I had was the phone. Eventually we got adjoining apartments, which are connected by a door. At last we have our own phones in our own separate spaces."

"Do you think the history of the master/slave relationship has anything to tell us about relationships today?" I asked Foucault.

"Of course, a lot," he said. "Look at Marivaux on the subject."

"Marivaux? He would not immediately spring to my mind on this matter," I confessed.

"*L'Île des esclaves!*" Mike inserted pertly.

"Yes, that's it!" Foucault said. "Marivaux shows us in such a delightful way how much pleasure the slave gets when he has a good master. The masters want to become slaves; they try to become slaves."

As Foucault gathered his things together in preparation for departure, I asked him what he had enjoyed most since we returned from our trip through the looking glass.

"The morning in the mountains," he answered. "I loved the hike with the young men in Bear Canyon."

"We will send you a five-hundred-dollar check for your official engagements in Claremont," I assured Foucault.

"But you have provided me with so much already," he said softly.

"We have already been set aside your fee compliments of the European Studies Program," I said.

"So it would be just throwing money away," he remarked.

"Exactly."

"You live in a paradise here," Foucault said.

"Given the unsavory politics in this crummy university, it may become paradise lost for us," I replied. "In any case, I intend to hold to my persuasion that the role of the teacher has to change. In response to events, your work, and my own personal development, I have become very involved with my students, in a few cases even intimately. I do not conceal my personal life or convictions from my students, and I make every attempt to connect my life with my teaching."

"Yes," Foucault responded, "it is the only way."

"I would call it Greek," I said.

"Yes," he said, "it is Greek."

"When are you going back to Paris?" David inquired.

"In a few weeks."

"Directly?"

"No, I am stopping in New York for a few days."

"Do you like New York a lot?" David went on.

"Yes, it is the city of cities."

"What do you like about it so much?"

"It is possible to become anonymous in New York. You can get your food from machines; you just put money into machines and get along without establishing any human contact."

"Do you stay in hotels?" Mike wondered.

"Yes, I try to stay in hotels that afford the greatest anonymity possible. I like hotels that give the feeling that you could be anywhere in the world."

"When can you come back and visit us?" David asked Foucault imploringly.

"Instead of stopping off in New York on my way back to Paris, I could come here for two days. I would like to spend some time with David in the mountains."

"Great idea," David exclaimed enthusiastically. Mike and I concurred.

WE REACHED THE WAITING ROOM, where we lingered until the flight was called.

"When you return," I said to Foucault, "would you appear on a TV series I am doing for the local CBS station? It is called *Claremont Colloquium* and I would like to begin my segment of shows with an interview with you."

He consented, albeit reluctantly. "I will do anything that will help you," he said.

"Have you appeared on television very much in France?" Mike asked.

"The authorities will not let me. Oh, they will let me on a program dealing with some innocuous subject, such as a dialogue about a book or some esoteric topic relating to school curriculum. I have done both. But to speak about prisons or politics or anything of significance, not a chance. The French power system guards access to the media very carefully," Foucault concluded.

"What do you think of American TV?" Mike asked him.

"A moral sermon! On American TV especially, people just play roles to satisfy the people who are watching. But it is interesting from the standpoint that it gives you a window on the viewers' problems. I saw an episode of a soap opera recently where the lady gets a face-lift to impress her husband. All her friends comment on how beautiful the face-lift was. But her husband doesn't recognize that anything has happened and she's so let down!"

"It didn't used to be that way when I was a kid," Mike said. "I was nurtured by *Our Miss Brooks, The Outer Limits, Lost in Space, Gumby,* and so many other shows. Not to mention the late-night movies."

"Do you feel like you are playing a role when you are on TV?" David interjected.

"Yes. That I am being directed to play a role. I felt that way when I was interviewed on TV with Noam Chomsky. He is a very kind man, but we were made to assume roles, which were moreover totally inaccurate."

"So you do not underestimate the power of the media?" asked David.

"On the contrary," said Foucault. "We live in two worlds: the inner world, the personal world, which is made up of our immediate, sensible experience, and the outer world, which we are not directly able to communicate with. It is communicated to us by the media— the newspapers, television, and the like. But it is communicated in a very distorted way."

"For example," Foucault continued, "not long ago I saw a copy of *Time* magazine from the year 1945. I lived through the events that *Time* magazine purported to represent. But the events were completely distorted by the *Time* editors. All you have to do is to live through what the story is supposed to be about, then read the story, and you will get a good idea of the distortions. We have to be able to convey our own story, to record and communicate the stories from our childhood, our life. In this way we can overcome the distortion of the outer world foisted upon us by the media."

"But how can we avoid depending so much on television for our stories?" inquired Mike.

"Take advantage of the latest technology. With the VCR and the video cameras you can make your own shows, tell your own stories, and exchange them with your friends."

For the plane Foucault carried a Zola novel. I gave him Mailer's *Armies of the Night* and a short story by Borges I had clipped from the *New Yorker*. It was titled "Utopia of a Tired Man."

"Michel," I said, "I am really looking forward to our television show together."

"Oh, really," he said with a tone of incredulity. "Why?"

"I want everyone to see you as a person."

"But I am not a person," Foucault responded sharply.

"All right, as a human being."

"That's worse," Foucault said with a laugh.

Then I saw with my own eyes what he was saying. As Foucault hugged and kissed us goodbye he metamorphosed successively into the Deleuzian becomings: child, woman, marmoset, leopard, crystal, orchid, water lily, stammerer, nomad, stranger, intense music, and finally, his ultimate dream, imperceptible.

"We have had many pleasures together," he said, as if from afar. His eyes glistened with the radiance of Venus rising over Zabriskie Point. Foucault molecularized into the arms of his men and then he was gone.

ABOUT THE AUTHOR

Simeon Wade was born July 22, 1940, in Alabama. After earning his Ph.D. in the intellectual history of Western civilization from Harvard in 1970, he moved to California and became an assistant professor at Claremont Graduate School. Wade later taught at several universities in Southern California and worked as a psychiatric nurse. He died in Oxnard, California, on October 3, 2017.

Heather Dundas is a Ph.D. candidate in literature and creative writing at the University of Southern California.

www.ingramcontent.com/pod-product-compliance
Lightning Source LLC
Jackson TN
JSHW081317130125
77033JS00011B/329